I0156351

THE TESTICLE KING

By: Ryan Walz

This book is dedicated to all my beautiful people: my incredible wife, Nichole; the best father a man could ask for, Bob; and my five beautiful children-never forget the power that lives within your hearts. To Kami for all the wonderful memories. And to all the amazing people along the road.

TESTICUZZI
for the nuts

Introduction:

Welcome to my fucked-up, wild-ass ride of a book, proof you can stack millions, lose your soul, and snatch it back, all by staring down the universe and daring it to blink, shaping reality with your mind. I'm Ryan, Testicle King, ex-Mormon, empire-builder, sinner, lover, dad--I've lived it raw, no filter. This isn't some polished self-help sermon or a sanctimonious sob story, it's a messy, pervy dump of how I turned thoughts into a $10 million deal, from a Provo basement to viral gold with Testicuzzi – that hot tub for your nuts -- with pit stops at swinging parties, nanny scandals, and a family I nearly lost but won back. Spoiler: the law of attraction is real. My mind turned chaos into cash and my crumbling family into a living-room hug worth more than any jet. I'm proof: own your story, scars and all, and you shape the life you want.

Forged in Mormon steel— tithing envelopes, mission calls, temple guilt, I broke free, excommunicated and unshackled, chasing a life that didn't bow to old ways. I hustled storage units into millions, flipped houses with dirt under my nails, and laughed as *Testicuzzi*, yes, that gem, raked in viral gold. But the ride got rough: partners stabbed me in the back, Nichole's family fanned the divorce flames, and my world teetered on the edge. It was my raw, unshakable belief— trust in a future I couldn't yet touch—that yanked us back from the edge. Bob, my rock, saw it; I saw it: kids laughing, love stitched back together, whole again. Through the wreckage—betrayal, fury, tears—I got it: what you focus on, you get. Gold or garbage, triumph or trash—your lens creates your reality.

This book? Evidence lived, not preached. Authors like Hicks and Goddard lit my fuse; now I'm torching the path my way, twisted, loud, unapologetic. *Saints of the Future* ain't a church with steeples, it's an idea: believe, receive, share. No pews, no dues, just you, me, maybe a field, some beers, and a fuck-you to fear. Join if you want, every soul's welcome, or just read this and run with it. Either way, I've done it – millions, miracles, messes – and you can, too. Buckle up—this shit's real.

Chapter 1: The Birth of a King

Chapter 2: The Kings Kingdom

Chapter 3: Missionary Style

Chapter 4: A new Heaven

Chapter 5: Boats and Tows

Chapter 6: For the Nuts

Chapter 7: The Nanny

Chapter 8: The lone King

Chapter 1:

The Birth of a King

You're probably wondering, *Who the hell is this guy, and why's he dubbed the Testicle King?* Well, buckle up, you're about to find out. This book might be the best damn thing you've ever read, or it might be a total trainwreck. Either way, we're in it now, and I'm not slowing down. Fair warning: I don't give a rat's ass what you think. Love it? Sweet. Hate it? Fine by me. But keep reading, and you'll get my unfiltered saga—a life so wild it'll stick with you, like it or not. I win either way.

It all kicked off in 1987, when I popped into the world as a screaming baby in Utah, Mormon country. Before my tiny feet even touched the ground, a chain of events I wouldn't note until almost thirty years later was already in motion. Picture this: a lusty young woman, probably where I get my own wild streak, hooks up for a threesome with two teenage cousins. The result? Me; one of the most insane, untamed, and flat-out successful bastards to ever walk the earth. That's not hype; it's fact, and you're about to see why.

I don't remember being born. Shocker, right? Truth is, I barely recall much of my childhood, either. Some say it's trauma from being ripped from my biological mom at birth, but I don't linger on that shit. I don't know and I don't care. What I *do* know is that every twist and turn hammered me into who I am, and I fucking *love* myself, a lot.

 My wife tries to soften me for others, saying stuff like, "Oh, he's not as cocky as he seems," or "He didn't mean it that way." She's half-right, sure, but it pisses me off when she apologizes for me being me. I get it, though not everyone digs confidence, not my kind. People mix it up with arrogance all the time. Here's the deal: I love myself, but I don't think I'm above anyone. I love others just as much, even the ones who rub me wrong. My mission?

Spot the good in every soul, that spark—call it God, the Universe, whatever—burning in me too. We're all lit up with it.

After I shot out of the cosmic portal—yep, a woman's vagina—baby me landed with Bob and Michelle Walz, courtesy of LDS Social Services. That's the Mormon church, slickly rebranded as The Church of Jesus Christ of Latter-day Saints because "Mormon" started smelling like a PR headache. They hooked up adoptions like mine, but by 2014, they bailed—too chickenshit to keep placing kids with a mom and a dad and catch flak for it. Just another checkmark on my list of bullshit Mormon decisions.

As a kid, I was fed Book of Mormon tales about badass dudes serving God. Take Abinadi, he faced persecution so brutal it'd make your skin crawl, torched alive in a fire. But God had his back; Abinadi strolled out of the flames unscathed, preaching repentance to the assholes who lit the match. That kind of story fired me up as a kid, stand for what you believe, no matter the cost, and with enough faith, you might just dodge the BBQ.

Yet the Mormon church? It was too busy dodging PR flames with politically correct backpedaling.

If I were the prophet, I'd be up on a mountain roaring, "Fuck you, gays, you're not adopting our Mormon babies!" not shuttering agencies to duck the fight. The crazy thing is, that would come from a place of love. I've got no issue with gay people, like I can love my wife and still disagree with her, I can disagree with their lives without joining the parade. But this underground Mormon "tolerance" bunch? They're not Mormons, they're morons. They swear God nuked Sodom and Gomorrah for sodomy, yet somehow, He's cool with all the gays now. Pick a damn lane. If you're gay, you're not Mormon; you're gay. Walk away from a God who smoked your ancestors (lol, ancestors).

Me? I don't care either way, but the church's flip-flops crack me up. "Unchanging, eternal God," they say, yet blacks couldn't hold the priesthood till '78, polygamy was holy, then heresy, and marrying 14-year-olds was fine when the founders did it. Their God's "unchanging" mind changes when the heat's on.

So yeah, LDS Social Services hooked me and my first adopted brother up with Bob and Michelle Walz, my new family.

Bob Walz, my dad, is the best father a guy could want. We see the world through different lenses, and that's fine, but one thing's rock-solid: even when our differences sparked disagreement, his love for me and mine for him never wavered. That's what counts. Bob, aka Robert Walz, was KSL TV's Utah County News Correspondent. a wannabe anchorman with a killer quip: "I could've been anchorman if I'd just had better eyebrows." He filled in sometimes, but those threadbare brows? Total dealbreaker.

Didn't matter-- he wasn't meant for the anchor desk. Bob scored bigger titles, like Utah County's Sexiest Man Alive. Dick Norris, some hotshot KSL anchor, couldn't touch that. Dick had the cash, sure, but Bob owned the ladies' hearts, and in my book, that's the real win. People said he looked like David Bowie or Robert Redford, which pissed me off as a teen when my cute friend swooned over him. Lesson learned: girls dig older guys.

Bob was a machine chasing breaking news or serving the Mormon ward as Bishop wrangling 150-600 souls like a general straight out of Doctrine and Covenants 107:68. Mom, Michelle, thrived as Primary President, "teaching" kids (brainwashing, says 40-year-old me). Relief Society ran the women, Elders Quorum herded the old guys—Bob oversaw it all, the sin-confession kingpin. He was my bishop for a decade, the guy I confessed my teenage sins to—like groping my girlfriend's chest over her shirt, awkward as hell.

I'm long gone from The Church of Jesus Christ of Latter-day Saints now, and I've got beef with its baggage. Still, it's not all trash—every system's got its highs and lows. It's no "one true church" to me, but it forged the Testicle King and sparked Saints of the Future (more on that later). The bad shit? That's what tempered the steel.

In Mormon Primary and Sunday School, Mom and the kids ate up the *Children's Songbook*—268 catchy little tunes for the flock. Take #78, "*I'm trying to be like Jesus, I'm following in his ways. I'm trying to love as he did, in all that I do and say. At times I am tempted to make a wrong choice, but I try to listen as the still small voice whispers, 'Love one another as Jesus loves you.'"* Sweet, right? Or #146, "Keep the Commandments": *"Keep the commandments, in this there is safety, in this there is peace."* Then #148, "I Want to Live the Gospel": *"I'll try to keep the commandments… to show that I am worthy, to live with him someday."* And #86, "The Golden Plates," hinting that Mormon Church founder Joseph Smith alone was "worthy" of God's confidence; yeah, so worthy he married 14-year-old girls. Song #162, "I Will Be Valiant," turns us into God's foot soldiers doing grunt work. Cute melodies, sure, but dig deeper and you see they're messed up. The message? *You're not like Jesus yet. You're unworthy unless you prove it. Screw up, and you're toast.* That's not what Jesus taught—it's the opposite. Real power's in loving yourself, not begging for approval.

Check John 8 in the Bible. Pharisees drag an adulteress to Jesus, itching to stone her per Mosaic Law, testing if He'll defy it. Jesus draws in the dirt, "He that is without sin among you, let him first cast a stone." Boom—convicted, they slink off.

Alone with her, He asks, "Where are your accusers?" She says, "Gone." He says, "Neither do I condemn thee: go, and sin no more." No probation, no checklist, Jesus says she's *worthy*, right then. Jesus didn't preach "Be like me"; He said "Do like me." Religions, Mormonism included, twist this subtly. "I'm *trying* to be like Jesus" implies you're not already there, that worthiness is a grind, not a gift. I call bullshit and reject that hard. Jesus knew we're all like Him: same spark, same potential, you just gotta act on it. That shift birthed the Testicle King. Those Primary songs? They planted the seeds of my rebellion.

Growing up Mormon, the pressure was weird as hell. Catch a glimpse of porn? Guilt tsunami, unworthiness so heavy it would paralyze. But desiring a naked woman? That's *natural*. Reconciling that tore me up. I'd overhear others speaking "unholy" talk and I'd judge them as trash, unrighteous losers. Gossip always flew: *"So-and-so cheated, what a disgrace,"* or *"Nancy's girl got knocked up!,"* the same shit that hit my biological mom. Late teens, pregnant from a threesome with two cousins (I still don't know which one's my dad), she got shipped off to hide the "shame." Mormonism's flaw—hell, most religions'--they bury shame deep instead of facing it. With the church sitting on $100 billion-plus cash pile, a real estate empire humming, why admit a damn thing? No one's crashing that gravy train. I can't crack open their books, but I've lived their culture. Sexual shame, unworthiness--that's their fruit from a poisonous tree. Those "slightly skewed" twists on Christ's teachings? They're at the root of it all.

I grew up on the west side of Provo, the poor side. The east side was where the rich flaunted their wealth. Dad, the news reporter, pulled in decent cash, but Mom, the ultimate penny-pincher, swore we were one skipped meal from the gutter. "We're broke," she'd preach, while shopping at thrift stores, clipping coupons, and plotting vacations to relatives' couches to dodge hotel bills. It never sat right with me. Outside our walls, I saw excess, people thriving; yet inside our walls, we were "starving."

Dad didn't play into it. Since he earned the dough, he'd sneak us treats, burgers, new kicks--quietly flipping Mom the bird. We'd join his rebellion, buzzing off the thrill of a forbidden Big Mac. That dopamine jolt from spending what we "shouldn't" lit a fuse in me. Dad wasn't wrong; it was *his* money. But sneaking it? That's the Mormon kid trap, burying natural urges instead of owning them. Mom's frugality wasn't her fault; her Mormon roots branded spending was sin. She couldn't see past it. Most can't. Asking "why" gets you shamed, not praised--church, government, society, take your pick. Spot a crack in the system? Good luck. People cling to their denial like life rafts, terrified to change. That's where I broke free.

As a kid, I burned to create and innovate. Couch forts and pretend games weren't enough—I craved more. Then in 1995, the Oklahoma City bombing hit. Dad's TV gig meant news was our nightly ritual, catching him on screen. That blast? Gutted buildings, shattered lives—not a move, but real as hell. At the age of eight, it broke me. I had to act. But we were "strapped" and miles away, what could I do? Then it came to me: popcorn. Sell it, send the cash to help. So I popped it, bagged it, and hit the streets like a pint-sized hustler, hawking to

14

neighbors. I had no clue how much I made--probably less than the shipping cost--but I buzzed with life. I had helped, somehow. Did Mom send it? She's stingy, but I'll bet she did. That was my first taste of entrepreneurial juice, roaming free, turning nothing into something. Other days, I'd haul my grandpa's war chest in my red wagon, stuffed with magic tricks, dazzling the neighborhood. That creative itch? It was waking up.

Dad's local fame rubbed off on me early. I picked up his PR swagger, hand gestures, charm, the works. In school, reading aloud was my stage; I'd nail it like a pro, soaking up praise for my delivery. But having a local celeb as a dad wasn't all rosy. Big news didn't care about holidays. Dad was gone a lot, chasing stories. This stung seeing dad most of the time sitting at a pulpit or through a TV screen. I loved the time I got to spend with dad, but him not being home much, it's what's shaped my relationship with my children today. Always home, always available. No pixels between us, no church calling holding me from serving my family.

There was some upside when I got to tag along. Hanging out with him and his cameraman, getting press passes to New Year's Eve gigs felt like Hollywood, and it gave my kid ego a fat boost. Everyone knew Bob Walz. Grocery runs turned into fan meet-and-greets, ten people minimum stopping him to chat about the latest headline. If it wasn't TV fame, it was "Bishop!" yells. Yeah, he was the sin-confession guy, but also the guy who loved you, cared about your mess, a dad to grown-ups. People adored him; he adored them back. I'd tag along for service gigs, mowing old ladies' lawns, dropping food to the jobless. Dad wasn't home as much as I wanted, but he was a damn Christ-like figure, always helping, always serving. That hustle, that charisma, that love? I owe him for wiring it into me.

Mom was a service junkie too, pouring time and soul into anything church-related. That's part of the baggage I lug from Mormonism. Callings don't just take time; they hijack it, borderline family theft. Sure, Monday was "family night," and we'd pile into church together, but the ward became our "family". Community's nice, but it stole real bonding--Mom prepping Sunday school lessons instead of tossing a ball with me, Dad serving the flock, not us. Noble? Maybe. But Mormons drown in it; their identity fuses with the collective hive; personal moments, quiet dinners with just us, got sidelined. Sunday services, weekly youth nights, and endless meeting—it creeps in. "Every member a calling", their mantra, keeps you sprinting on a hamster wheel of "do more." It's never enough.

At 18, you're guilted into a two-year mission; mine was Uruguay Montevideo West. Slack off? You're trash, nothing. Mormons are trained to feel they are never "enough," so they overdo it. It's a machine, a madhouse spitting out killer salesmen. Utah's a door-to-door sales empire—hustle's baked into the culture. Productive as hell, but balance? They've never heard of it. Like a bloated government with cash to burn, dreaming up programs, Mormons have too many hands and too many meetings, always plotting the next "must-do."

It's never been "enough"—not as a kid, and not now. It's a curse that keeps me restless; a rocket booster that won't let me sit still. My engine's always revving. If you tell me something's wrong just 'cause you *say so*, and show no proof? Watch out, that dynamite in me ignites. You're like my Mom swearing we're too broke to go to the movies even though I've peeked at the bank statement. Guess what? I'm going, and I'm watching that flick. You can't stop me. It's not rebellion for kicks; it's me demanding real talk, real facts. Dodge that, and you're a liar, a puppet twitching on some system's strings—done in my book. Dead to me. That clash, that fire, it's what forged me. I took "never enough", flipped it into fuel, and built my own damn path.

I grew up on Provo's west side till ten—gritty, broke, scrappy. Then we'd roll up to the east bench, Grandpa Walt and Grandma Myrle's world of big houses, boats, excess—a few miles away but another galaxy. Walt was a rocket scientist, Lockheed Martin vet, sharp till 103, when age finally dulled him. In those last years, black suits checked monthly to lock down his secrets, but he spilled to me—stuff Mom never heard. Lunar Lander? He built it. Advised presidents? Yup. Patents on analog computers, planes, his name's on 'em. Dropped Project BAMBI too—a '50s plot to park satellites with mini-missiles in orbit, blasting Soviet ICBMs (intercontinental ballistic missiles) at launch. He'd grin: "We could shoot rockets from space back then." Blew my mind. North Korea's flexing? Nuclear panic? Bullshit—Grandpa's tech had it covered decades ago.

I'd push him, *"Grandpa, what's the deal?"* Too many questions, and he'd clam up, eyes darting. I'd tease, "You just not allowed to say?" He'd nod. I begged him to stash a book of secrets for me. "You'll be dead, what's it matter?" He passed in 2024, no book. Project BAMBI's real, though—Google and AI confirm it, an Air Force dream scrapped 'cause $500 million (in today's money) per satellite was nuts, and Soviets could bankrupt us with decoys. Patents check out, too; Walt's fingerprints dot aviation history. I'm no conspiracy freak—just a kid who questions. Aliens? Bob Lazar, Area 51—I've binged it all. "Real, Grandpa?" Silence. *That was my answer.* That hush, plus BAMBI's wild truth, lit my fuse to doubt everything and woke my rebel soul. Grandma Myrle, his hardworking sweetheart, was my first gut-punch loss when she passed. We'd kill hours with Uno— she banned face cards as the devil's tools, called the Beatles Satan's crew. Rock-solid old soul, that woman—she stuck to her guns, and it sparked my grit.

Dad's dad, John Walz, was an Idaho farmer-accountant who survived Okinawa in WWII but came back scarred—PTSD screaming fits, haunted eyes. Who could blame him after that hell? They'd settled in California by then, and it crushed Dad when John died there in his fifties. Bob was a kid carrying that weight, so he swung hard the other way—no barking orders, just love, maybe too soft. Funny how trauma ricochets. Losing John in his twenties gutted Bob, still does, but it shaped him into the good guy, never the hard-ass. Dad's mom, Grandma Jeanie, was the heart he drew from— pure sunshine, sweetest soul alive. Ask about John, she'd twinkle, "I don't speak ill of the dead." Even when shingles hit late, she'd clutch her chest, "Not getting fresh—just hurts!" Pain couldn't dim her; she'd still crack you up. Heaven's VIP, no question.

Before my parents knew I'd be theirs, John (long passed on) came to Jean in a dream and said, "*Ryan's coming.*" Epic—an honor from beyond, him picking me. After John's death, Jean left California for Utah, chasing her kids to BYU's snowy Mormon bubble. There, she remarried Grandpa Gordon, a gent straight out of a black-and-white flick. Treated her like gold—every car door opened, never saw her touch a handle. Gordon? Howard Hughes's right-hand man—yep, the half-mad Aviator genius (watch it, I won't spoil). John's war grit, Gordon's tales, Walt's rocket secrets—my grandpas handed me a jackpot of wild shit, pushing me to question, to hustle.

My childhood was a scrappy proving ground, a warmup for the real game. Those east-side Provo glimpses of big, beautiful houses and lavish excess were about to go from daydreams to my daily reality at age ten. Grandpa Walt and Grandma Myrle, his rock-solid old soul, ditched the hilltop home for St. George's sun—Mormon turf, hot as Hades, less snow. They offered their pad to their six kids; Bob and Michelle snatched it. Boom—the rich side wasn't a visit; it was home.

Chapter 2:

The King's Kingdom

I woke up one morning in a second-hand king-size bed in my new bedroom, high on that east-side hill. It felt like a fresh start, a tangible upgrade. Twin bed to king, cramped shared room to my own sprawl. Big enough to breathe. The house sat across from a vacant field that'd become my playground--hours of football, night games, even some steamy makeout sessions with girl-friends. West to east wasn't just a move; it was a damn glow-up. The people talked differently: crisper, happier. They carried themselves like they belonged. The neighborhood buzzed with families like ours, ten to fifteen boys my age on deck, a leap from the two or four pals I'd had on the west side. Our living room flexed a vaulted ceiling and floor-to-ceiling windows, framing a grassy field with a mountain towering over us. A cave pocked its cliff face, too dicey to climb, but I'd stare, plotting. New kid nerves hit hard watching those field boys play, but I sucked it up, marched out, and bam, friends piled up fast. Mormonville perks: church glued us together. Sunday School, Boy Scouts, youth nights, extra excuses to vibe with the crew. The real prize? Girl-spotting events.

Life from ten onward burns clear in my head; before that, it's a fog. Family, especially my wife, gnaw at why—trauma, maybe? I don't care. Whatever happened, happened, digging up ghosts won't change me now. Still, weird flicker lingers from west Provo. Near our old place, Geneva Steel ran a park, killer spot with a real locomotive engine bolted to tracks. Kids climbed it, yanking levers--some welded, some loose--teasing you into thinking you'd roll it. A stream meandered through, bridges arched, gazebos hugged the hillside, paths wound past picnic tables. Then, hazy as hell, this memory: some creep asking me to flash my junk. That's it, my memory cuts out. I've told my wife; she digs, but I've got zilch. Mentioned it to Dad once, and he dropped, "Yeah, that happened, we got you therapy." Shocked me silent. Later, I pushed again; he backpedaled, "Maybe that was another kid in the ward." What the hell?

It's a muddle I don't sweat much. Truth's elusive, and I'm done chasing it. But it stinks religion's rot, society's too: molestation, rape, sexual filth, rampant, yet hushed like the sin is in saying it. I don't know if that park moment scrambled my early recall, but it steers how I raise my kids now--open doors, no dark corners. More later. For now, teenage Ryan Walz.

My best pals from that east-side crew were twins, Adam and Jared, sons of Jim and Linda, a knockout mom of six, two twin sets, heart of gold. My second mom; I practically lived there. Linda fed and wrangled the whole neighborhood, tolerance off the charts; that is, until some kid's dumbass move flipped her switch, and boom, playtime's over. I'd be hoofing it home. Adam's still my ride-or-die. He's got a heart like Linda's and a self-deprecating humor that'll crack you up; we'd tease he got 30% of the womb's cells, Jared snagging 70%. No one's ever made me laugh harder; his awkward, genius shtick is gold. Picture us in a theater, him chucking popcorn at strangers, pinning it on some rando. Trouble magnet--I loved it.

Adam, Jared, me, and the neighborhood posse, we were chaos incarnate, Jackass-level stunts deserving of a VHS deal. Wish we could dig up those tapes. We staged a fake kidnapping once--shoved Adam in a friend's trunk, slammed it, all on camera, dreaming of MTV glory. Later, in some random hood, he'd yank the emergency release, bolt, and we'd chase him down--masked, bats swinging, "beating" him, tossing him back in. The cops weren't amused, but we were kids, so we dodged the cuffs. We'd rejig traffic cones in construction zones, harmless, pure kicks. Days bled into nights in the gully, crafting a paintball warzone, layered up like tanks, dishing pain like champs. Post-Christmas, we'd hijack a buddy's dad's truck, snatch discarded trees, and cram, oh, forty?—into some sucker's unlocked living room. We never stuck around for the fallout, but picturing their WTF face? Priceless. Egging? TP-ing? Lame. We craved different.

One rich pal's remodel had a porta-potty—prime target. Tipping it was basic, but we made it war. We'd drive by, cackling, wondering how long 'til they'd right it. My masterpiece? Nailing it with my '93 Jeep Wrangler--a perfect corner shot. It crumpled, sprang back, then launched a hundred feet down the street. Wildest damn thing I'd seen. Their response? They chained it down with cum-alongs and metal straps, like it was guarding the apocalypse. That tethered porta-potty was our trophy—we'd pushed 'em there. That rush, that defiance? Pure Testicle King fuel.

Moving from west-side Provo to the east didn't just score me Adam, Jared, and the gang--it flung me into a new orbit. West-side folks were modest, hardworking, salt-of-the-earth. But these east-side titans? Doctors, lawyers, CEOs, sales sharks.. Church and Boy Scouts fused tightly back then; youth nights doubled as merit badge hunts, and damn near all us boys walked out Eagles. Those skills, those memories? Whole books' worth. These guys had what west-siders didn't: resources, time, vision. Living there was a daily TED Talk, and I soaked it up.

Home teaching, a church gig where you'd check
on three families post-Sunday, paired me with
legends. Scott, VP of American Stores—a multibillion-dollar grocery-drug empire in the '90s and
a bigwig at Fidelity Charitable, rolled up weekly.
This wasn't some nobody; he'd grab me, we'd visit
our families, then he'd buy me a Jamba Juice and
riff business gold. Distribution, supply-demand, in-
ventory traps: too much stock jacks storage costs,
too little kills sales. I soaked it up like a sponge
while others shelled out fortunes for that wisdom.
One day, he drove me an hour to Salt Lake, we
hit a Wendy's, and he pointed out the drive-thru.
"Highest-grossing in the state, maybe the country," he said. Why? They'd cracked a system to
sling cars through faster than anyone. My heart
swells for Scott, his kindness shaped me. Then
there's Dee, insurance ace and real estate mogul.
Dee put me to work, mowing his rental yards for
cash while dishing sales wisdom on the drives.
Best tale? A salesman mailed a shoe to a stubborn
client with a note: "Can't get my foot in the door,
call me." Landed a whale. Dee even hooked me up
with sales books. The universe saw my hunger for

wealth and deal-making, and it delivered.

Boy Scout camp was next level insanity. Our ward's mad geniuses ditched standard camp sites for Lake Alexander in the Uintahs, a serene pine nook turned teenage Valhalla for two weeks. Leaders hauled trailers up early, built a tent city with bonkers perks: shooting ranges, a legit bathroom—flushing toilet, hot shower, pipes snaking through trees, a gourmet kitchen, even a 300-foot zipline from an old elevator cable one guy's company scrapped out of his building. Post-camp, they'd erase it all, Leave No Trace, Boy Scout style. I earned swimming, shooting, knot-tying, wilderness survival badges, rowed out to salvage a sunken boat, too. Mornings kicked off with a homemade cannon blast and bugle speakers rigged in the forest. Nights? Pyrotechnic wet dreams. They'd float a raft to the lake's center, a 20-foot pallet tower stuffed with fireworks, zip flaming bottle rockets from shore via tree cables to ignite it, and we'd watch that heap blaze to ash. Dutch oven desserts capped it. Only bummer? Wilderness survival night. We had to build a hut from sticks, sleep in it. Thank God for sleeping bags.

Pranks? Hell yes. My favorite: the "bear noise machine." Leaders cranked it, fired blanks, yelled "It's in the kitchen!"--my cue to bang pots like a grizzly was raiding. Newbies probably shit themselves; we laughed 'til it hurt. Those men, Scott, Dee, the camp crew—their selfless acts forged me. From business smarts to batshit creativity, they lit the fuse for my fire within.

Then Jerry, a hardcore bastard who lived for pain. His motto? "No near-death, no growth." While other leaders dished wisdom, Jerry served raw survival--brute strength, resilience forged in hell. We dreaded his reign, but damn, it stuck. Fifty-milers were his game. We'd craft snowshoes, trudge through subzero to build igloos, nights so brutal I'd pray for death. Reward? A fire, thaw one limb, freeze the other, repeat. He dragged us across deserts, up sand dunes, and down treacherous rivers, his favorite. Jerry snagged rare once-in-a-lifetime rafting permits, us Scouts in tow, body bag packed "just in case."

Those river trips, Green River to Lake Powell, were Jerry's trap; he'd con us into repeats. One trip, headwinds pinned us, 30 kayaks, rowing to nowhere. Our pickup crew roared upstream in a wakeboard boat, found us flailing, and towed us down, wind be damned. Another time, Adam, my fearless goofball, shone. Day three on killer rapids, we'd usually scout, park our rubber duckies (kayaks), hike the bank, map the safest path. Not him. Adam, cocky as hell, just went for it. I watched from shore as he vanished into monster waves--20 seconds stretched forever--then bam, his kayak's nose rocketed skyward over the drop, Adam flailing like a circus cannon shot him out. He crashed back beyond sight, unscathed. We laughed 'til it hurt, but most of us hiked around, his balls-out stunt was lesson enough. That image? My go-to chuckle fuel.

Jerry's death marches peaked when I volunteered for the cargo raft--overachiever bait. I craved the grind. Parker, a mentor, rode along, his sons in the mix. A week of near-drowning bonds you like war; respect runs deep. Back home, Parker cornered me at church. "Gear raft? That was an impressive hustle. Come work for me." Parker wasn't just rich; he was private jet rich, God-tier cash. I'd mowed lawns for west-side scraps; now I orbited a titan. My dreams of a big house, nice car were small fry. Jet money, funny money, that's the goal now. Parkers' vibe? Pure play. One day, post-shopping, he rolled up with a "body" in his trunk. "Strip it, ditch it in the dumpster," he said. We crept up, hearts pounding—found a plastic Santa. He'd bought it for the suit, for a Christmas party gag. West-siders would've cried "waste!" Parker? Laughed, then punked us into thinking we'd bury a corpse. Child-like, never cruel, he was just a big kid with cash.

Parkers' wealth freed him--humor, zero serious-ness--yet Mormon to the core. Bought an RV, ripped out the coffee maker to dodge any "hot drinks" whiff (Mormons can't have hot drinks). I'd have kept it for hot water, but Parker? Hardcore. That mix, playful excess, iron faith, blew my mind. Jerry taught me to survive; Parker showed me to thrive. Both sparked the Testicle King.

Parker had a gaggle of kids, but one daughter, right around my age, hooked me. She was stunning, sun-kissed hair catching the light, a charming grin that could melt ice. Going to Parker's was heaven every day: hard grind under a wide sky, lessons sinking in deep, big laughs, and those fleeting glimpses of her flitting around. I was too shy, too damn innocent to make a move, heart thudding, palms sweaty. I just nursed it quietly in my head, a fun flicker to chew on during long shifts. Funny twist? Her cousin was my first kiss—sassy, sharp. That kiss was a mess, me fumbling, lips awkward, her and her pals cackling after, "What was that?" I burned red, but it stuck with me early: don't let flops define you. I leveled up, kissing skills honed sharp, plenty of grins to prove it.

At Parkers', I rolled with Matt and Michael--older guys, bosses on paper, brothers in the dirt. They carried Parker's vibe: work hard, play harder, live loud. We'd tackle wild jobs and turn 'em into a riot. One summer day, I'm perched in a tractor bucket, makeshift seat bolted on, wobbling under me, frying in the high sun on Parkers' mountain spread. The land stretched out raw, pine thickets clawing the slopes, dust swirling in the breeze, views slamming your chest like a fist. A 500-gallon tank of weed killer sloshed behind, hose snaking to a sprayer in my grip, and me blasting thistle.

Parker hated that prickly bastard, wanted it gone so horses could gallop free or four-wheelers could rip trails without snagging. Matt's sat in the air-conditioned cab, cool as a cucumber, while I was out there, sweat stinging my eyes, days blurring into a haze of spray and heat. Miserable? Sure. Fun? Hell yeah--Matt's grin through the glass, our shouted jabs over the roar, turned it into sport. We'd clean storm drains, mud sucking at our boots, scoop dog shit from kennels, flies buzzing, and even wrestle busted toilets 'til porcelain gleamed. Still, I felt like the luckiest bastard alive, rubbing elbows with Parker daily, soaking it all in.

Parker's crew mirrored him, loose, loud, alive. Matt and Michael blasted Motley Crue from a battered speaker while we hauled lumber, wrestled pipes, sweat drenching our shirts like a second skin.

Parker would toss nuggets—pure gold, off-hand--"Sometimes you just work harder than the next guy," squinting at the horizon. I scribbled it down in a beat-up notebook, ink smudging my fingers, and reviewed em like holy writ under my bedroom lamp. But what he didn't say taught more. Parker wasn't the one scrubbing toilets or drowning in thistle spray, he'd climbed past that. His hands stayed clean while ours blistered. Wealth has phases: grind 'til you're raw, then rise above it. When I wasn't at school, or church, hymns droning, or working, I'd read like a fiend. I was voracious as hell--*Art of the Deal*, Trump's brash growl; *Rich Dad Poor Dad*, Kiyosaki's cash gospel; *The Millionaire Mind, Think and Grow Rich*, pages dog-eared, spines cracked.

Now, I knock out 20 books a year, minimum, jet fuel for the brain. Knowledge is power, get it? I saw it young: broke folks griped, sour as old milk; rich ones spoke possibility, bright as dawn. Positivity breeds success, not the other way around. Naysayers stay stuck in their mud-caked boots; optimists climb, kicking the dirt off. Later, I'd know it as the Law of Attraction. Parker was walking proof.

He was a jet-rich titan, crazy big money, but a kid inside, laughing at dumb jokes like me, eyes crinkling. Life was his sandbox with no edges. When

Crocs dropped—ugly, rubber clogs nobody wanted—he tossed me a bright orange pair (think traffic
cone), fresh from the launch. "Next big thing," he
grinned. "Wear 'em proud." It was a weird, tough
ask, neon screaming on my feet, kids snickering,
but I rocked 'em, soles slapping pavement, head
high. Not daily--God, no--but enough. Later, I
snagged gray pair, wore 'em regularly, a quiet
badge. The lesson hit: own who you are, swagger
in anything, rags or riches.

Adam and Jared, my ride-or-die twins, suited up
for the football team, shoulder pads clacking, turf
dust kicking up under stadium lights. Not me. I
was wired differently, restless, and I always knew
it deep in my gut. Jocks are beasts--sweat-soaked
bad-asses-- But it's not my lane. What bugs me?
Bleacher zombiesI never got it, life's a wide-open
sprawl, bursting with shit to do, and I can't wrap
my head around wasting hours cheering some
dude living his dream on the big stage. If you're an
athlete watching the greats, studying moves, that's
sharp. But the "lucky" socks guy, stinking of beer,
yelling at the TV like it matters? Nah. Life's too
big to rerun someone else's script.

Sure, there's something to be said about the audience fueling the game. Those gridiron gods might not charge so hard without the roar of the stands, the sea of painted faces howling their names. But life's a video game, and I see it clearly: there's non-player characters—NPCs—shuffling through, men and women just doing what they're told, heads down, waiting for the bell. They don't ask why, don't dream differently. Like extras in a movie, milling in the background while the real story rolls. Me? I'm the main fucking character, joystick in hand, carving my own damn path through the pixels.

If you're reading this, nodding along saying, "Shit, that's me", don't beat yourself up. This is your wake-up call. Shake off that heavy coat of "who you've been", and see it: a new trail's blazing right in front of you, dirt fresh under your boots, ready for a whole new life you can build with your own hands.

While Adam and Jared punted footballs across muddy fields, I stacked cash at sixteen slinging for Parker. Perk? Endless. Money buys damn near everything. I turned into a machine, a dating beast, Jeep Wrangler growling through Provo streets, matte black with a stereo thumping bass so hard the windows rattled. Chicks dug it—heads turning, hair flipping, me in Spyder jackets, Rossignol skis racked, Motorola Razr snapping open, then the first iPhone glowing slick. Dates? Steakhouses, sizzling plates; movies, plush seats, buttery popcorn. Money talks, money frees— that lesson carved itself deep in my bones.

I'd noted it earlier: women crave older guys, Bob's charm taught me that, but Parker's world proved why. They want to be taken care of; they want steaks, soft lights, a rock—safety over broke, fumbling young dudes. But me? I was the outlier. Young, but no fool scraping pennies. Braces clamped my teeth and acne speckled my face like a war zone, but cash and swagger smoothed it. When those braces came off, teeth straight, skin clear– paired with my money and success? I couldn't rotate girls fast enough. Girlfriends? A few (more on that later), but Dad laid down a rule: one different date a week, no repeats. I loved it, kept me loose, sampling the field like a buffet. Tried holding that rule later; my wife's not as keen, her eyes rolling when I float it. Dad's play was smar—don't lock in too soon, chains chafe—and I'm already drilling it into my teenage boys over pancakes. Settle when it's time, not before. Dating all kinds—shy, loud, flirty—honed my game, taught me the moves.

But super Mormonism loomed, a shadow over my strut. It was that mission thing–two years serving God, preaching Jesus in some far-off corner, home a memory. Calls allowed twice a year, Mother's Day and Christmas, voices crackling over static. It hung there, a weight on every high, youth nights, paintball welts, river rapids, all prep for that holy haul. Parker sweetened it: "Save for your mission fund, I'll match every buck." Gold deal–I'd rake cash hauling his gear, picturing crisp bills doubling in a jar. Brilliant, right? The church hooks you young, Sunday School songs, Scout oaths, raises you to expect that trek, then makes you pay for the privilege. Sure, wards chip in–donations subsidize plenty of kids–but with Parker's match, I bankrolled damn near my whole Uruguay stint—humid streets thick with yerba mate, dust in my lungs. Mom, the tightwad queen, must've beamed; her ledger clean. Still, while out there, my creative streak flared, antics needing extra dough, and Bob and Michelle ponied up, wiring cash to fuel my wild Montevideo hustle.

The problem was the pressure. God doesn't ask, he expects; it's a divine demand stamped on your soul like a cattle brand. Same deal with tithing, ten percent of your cash forked over monthly, no excuses, no wiggle room. It's not optional; it's the Mormon tax. Don't pay? You're out, your temple worthiness torched, no celestial VIP pass. Wanna marry a stunner like Parker's daughter, all grace and glow? Better serve that mission, kid. Here's the real grift, the Mormon hustle: you cough up ten percent of your money, coins clinking in the bishop's envelope, and then give at least ten percent of your time, hours bleeding into meetings and callings.. As a young kid steeped in Mormonville, surrounded by the faithful, pioneer stock in their veins, it's a mountain looming over you, shadow cold and heavy. Choice? What choice? Everyone's in, every man who mentored me punched that ticket: Dad trudging Michigan winters, Parker charming France with his grin, Scott and Dee with their own tales of mud and miracles. If I didn't go, I'd be unworthy, a tainted smudge among a sea of pressed white shirts.

The girls I dated–all Mormon–eyed returned missionaries (RM), the golden boys back from the field. Mormon girls marry Mormon boys, but not just any; RM status required, badge gleaming. Another perk for the older guys: ages 18 to 20 vanish, poof, gone to preach, leaving a two-year gap. Date a younger guy? He's shipping out, suitcase snapping shut; you're stuck penning letters, paper creasing under your grip, while he's off saving souls. Why cozy up to a ghost who's gonna bolt? Better chase the ones already back, ties loosened, stories spilling, mission glow still on 'em. I felt it, that clock ticking, girls sizing me up, knowing I'd either go or fade. The pressure's a vice, squeezing your chest 'til you nod yes, your future a script already penned in Salt Lake ink.

I've laid out the perks, the wild camps, the mentors like Parker matching my mission fund, doubling my stack with a handshake. That shit was gold, no lie. Those benefits I'll never knock, forged by men

41

and women who poured their hearts into the youth, their community. Parker's cash, Scott's Jamba Juice riffs, Dee's sales yarns, those came from living men, not the machine. But here's my take now: you don't need a church sucking ten percent of your green to pull that off. Those epic trips, Lake Alexander's ziplines, Jerry's death marches–church okayed 'em, sure–but they were "extra," bankrolled by guys dipping deeper into their own pockets, trucks loaded. The official ten percent? That's for the church buildings gleaming white marble, real estate piling high. Billions, maybe trillions, in holdings: chapels with steeples piercing the sky, basketball courts echoing with squeaking sneakers (Jesus loves hoops, right after football, profit dripping from both). Welfare programs feed some poor, sure, but then you've got mega malls sprouting like City Creek, its glass and neon clashing with the pioneer vibe. God says build a mall? Church snaps to it, hammer's down, no questions. And don't you dare ask why, just nod, smile, and pass the tithing tray.

I gotta be honest; at the time, I was all in. I was serving that mission, no question, picturing myself striding back a hero, white shirt crisp, tie knotted tight, ready to sweep Parker's daughter off her feet and into a Mormon fairy tale. Oh, the optimist, young and dumb, head full of dreams. Truth is, we barely knew each other. She was sweet, shy smile, eyes darting away–took her to a dance once, her dress swishing soft under gym lights, me awkward in a church suit, fumbling a corsage onto her wrist. But if I'm real, I've got no clue if she ever gave a damn about me. Super cute, sure, all quiet charm, but I hadn't cracked her code, didn't know her game; hell, I didn't even know mine. A handful of dates, ice cream dripping down cones, movie seats creaking, and that was it. Still, some spark in me thought, Maybe, just maybe.

Hindsight's a bitch. Plenty of guys probably drooled over marrying the rich man's daughter, her dad's jet-rich glow a magnet. My work buds, Matt and Michael, caught the vibe, they'd rib me over it, leaning on shovels, grinning through sweat. "Just go serve, kid," they'd say, voices echoing off Parker's barn. "Come back, you'll be set, ring on her finger, mansion keys in hand." Back then, I'd bet Parker would've loved it too, me, his golden boy, tying the knot with his girl.

See, Parker and my dad are thick as thieves, best buds forged in church pews. When one was bishop, the other played counselor, a pulpit tag-team trading spots, cracking wise from the pulpit—ties loosened, big laughs. It was a breath of fresh air in a church stuffed with uptight assholes and starched collars, pursed lips, judging eyes. Those two lightened the heavy air of hymnals and guilt. From stuff Dad dropped, casual, over dinner, fork scraping plate, and Parker's offhand nods, I got the sense they were hoping we'd click. Maybe her shy glances meant something, maybe not. I hoped it too, heart thumping when she'd pass by, her perfume trailing faint, but big shit was barreling my way, a freight train of somethings, and she wasn't on the passenger list. She wrote to me on the mission— sweet letters, smudged ink—but I couldn't read her, felt forced, like a pity pen. Who knows? Maybe she liked me. Maybe someday I'll ask, catch her eye at a reunion, truth spilling over coffee, I mean soda (Mormons don't drink coffee). She's got a beautiful family now, married to one of my buddy's brothers, solid guy—not the Testicle King, though, no crown, no chaos.

You want something wild? All that extra cash, flaunting hot dates, makeout sessions steaming up my Jeep's windows, tongues tangling under streetlights, and I was a virgin. Picture it: young, righteous Mormon boy, chest puffed, aiming for gold, celestial glory, not just a quick score. A few girls pushed hard, hands roaming, breath hot on my neck, and man, I'd throw the holy water, figuratively splashing 'em off like demons recoiling from a priest. They didn't take it well, eyes flashing hurt, lips tightening. Now I get it: a woman offers herself, you shove her back, it's not just "no thanks," it's her you're rejecting, a gut punch to the soul. The few who pressed, whispering in the dark, fingers tugging my shirt, didn't grasp the steel Mormon wall I'd built, forged in Sunday School and sacrament bread. I'm sure it stung, but it didn't faze me. I was worthy, untouchable, God's soldier polishing his armor. Their tears didn't dent me; I had a mission approaching.

That moment hit like a freight train. I'm in our living room, carpet worn from pacing feet. Dad's there, tie loose, Parker filming, my buddies, Adam, Jared, a few others sprawled on the couch, eyes locked on me. The envelope's in my hands, cream paper, crisp from Salt Lake, seal unbroken: my mission call, the Lord's marching orders. I rip it open, fingers trembling just a hair, and read it loud, voice steady but heart hammering: "Ryan Walz, the Lord has called you to serve in the Uruguay Montevideo West Mission (or as Parker would riff, "You're a Gay Montevideo"). You will report to the MTC in Provo, Utah, and depart for Uruguay two months later." Silence drops, then cheers, Dad clapping my back, Parker's grin splitting wide, and friends whooping like it's a touchdown. That was it, all the fun, the games, the shiny lessons from east-side titans, the cash-fueled swagger, it was time to pay the piper. God had been good, dishing out cash, girls, a Jeep growling through Provo nights, and now I'd pay Him back, boots on the ground, handing strangers the gospel like a lifeline in a storm.

I was willing, fists clenched, jaw set, but it scared the shit out of me, a raw ache twisting my gut. All that flash, iPhone gleaming sleek, Spyder jackets zipped tight against mountain wind, skis slicing powder on weekend runs, for what? For the next two years, it's a suit and tie, black polyester rubbing my neck raw, and one day a week, scrubs for a few precious hours off. Laundry spinning in a clanking machine, grocery bags rustling with rice, milk and soap, my big rebellion against the grind. I'd trade the Jeep's roar for my feet, the girls' perfume for sweat and dust, the high life for a cot in a cinderblock room, Spanish hymns echoing off cracked walls. Intense didn't begin to cover it. Every step to the MTC felt like shedding skin, leaving the king of Provo for a soldier of the Lord.

Chapter 3:

Missionary Style

I rolled into the MTC, the Missionary Training Center, solo, no familiar faces, just me and a duffel bag slung over my shoulder. It's smack in Provo, blocks from my teenage home, east-side streets I could trace blind. But there I was, locked in like a damn prisoner, razor wire replaced by faith and white brick walls. I'd peer out the window, grimy glass smudged from inside, and watch my friends cruise by, Jared's truck rumbling, Adam's laugh floating free, living the life I'd ditched. Me? Stuck, voluntarily, sure, but stuck all the same. Was it really voluntary? If I didn't chain myself in there, then slog two years in the field, I'd be trash, worthless in the Mormon game. No rich guy's daughter, hell, no guy's daughter. I was already celibate, braces off, acne fading; if I didn't lock it down, I might stay that way, a monk in a

Wrangler.

So the clock kicked off, two years, I could gut it out. Everyone swore it'd pay off, voices echoing: "Worth it in the end, Elder Walz." Day one, it began: study, study, study. Book of Mormon, leather cover creased; Bible, pages thin as whispers; Preach My Gospel, the missionary playbook; Doctrine and Covenants, rules stacking high. Oh, and Spanish, "Hola, señor, ¿dónde está el baño?", drilled into my skull 'til my tongue tripped. Two months to master it before a plane hauled me thousands of miles to a new world.

Provo taunted me–visible, close enough to taste, painful as hell. Most missionaries don't get that torture, training far from home, no familiar streets to haunt 'em. Me? I'd see my crew roll past daily, tires spinning free while I'm caged, flipping through scriptures under fluorescent buzz. Excruciating, a slow burn in my gut, but the countdown was on, and I'd push through, jaw set. Made some new pals quick–Joe and Ben squared up beside me in that MTC grind. Ben, I kinda knew, same high school, but we'd never clicked 'til now. Joe? California, el Norte, he'd say, flashing some goofy gang sign, a cool cat with a laugh that cut the gloom. Haven't talked to him in years–hope he's still kicking, still cracking wise. There we were, duped into locking ourselves in, a trio of suckers bonding over shared misery. Good news? Girls I'd dated sent care packages flooding in, cardboard boxes stuffed with cookies, gum, notes scribbled in girly loops. Even letters from Parker's daughter, her handwriting neat, envelope crisp with her custom artwork. Most missionaries don't realize it 'til later: that well dries fast. A few months, and the mail slows to silence.

Training dragged–Spanish verbs tangling my brain–then Montevideo hit. Prepared my whole life, books devoured nonstop, Book of Mormon and Bible a breeze, Spanish feeling solid in my mouth. Thought I had it down, swagger in my step. Boy, was I wrong. On the ground, it unraveled fast. On a mission, you're never solo, companion glued to your hip, shadows in sync. You sleep in the same room, cots creaking, snores bouncing off cinderblock, eat, preach, piss together. Whisper this quiet: the church's got some homosexuality static, and cramming two pent-up guys in a strange land? Shit gets shady. Not my scene, kept it straight–but a couple companions dropped lines, eyes glinting, voices low–that had me sleeping back-to-wall, just in case.

They shuffle you too, no settling in; every few months, new area, new face. Effective? Hell, if I know, but that's the drill. First stop: Montevideo, Uruguay's capital, streets alive with horns, vendors shouting, air thick with diesel and salt. My companion? Not American, not Uruguayan but Paraguayan, hailing from next door. He didn't speak my English, I didn't speak his Guarani; his Spanish outran mine, but barely fluent, choppy, accented. MTC Prep? Useless. Poof, no lifeline. I sank, syllables drowning me, Montevideo laughing at me.

Other Greenies stumbled; I learned fast. Had to. No choice, sink or swim in Montevideo's chaos. My companion, Elder Rojas, would lose it some days, barking at me in Guarani, his voice sharp as a machete, spit flying in the humid air. I'd yell back in English, lungs full, words bouncing off cracked walls, pointless, sure, but damn amusing. We'd stand there, red-faced, until Spanish kicked in, the only bridge between us. Funny twist? Later I found out he'd conned me, bus fares rattling in my pocket, taxi meters clicking, street food steaming in my hands, all my cash, when it was supposed to be split. Turns out Rojas was pocketing mission funds, heading back to Paraguay with a fat stack, probably a jackpot where he's from, enough to strut like a king. Not much sweat off my back; the guy was an asshole, sneaky smirk, always dodging chores, but since we jabbered in our own tongues, we hammered that Spanish hard. Took weeks, not months, 'til I had the basics—"¿Cuánto cuesta?", "Gracias, hermano"—rolling off my tongue. Now? Fluent as hell, years later, hiring workers from Mexico, Guatemala, El Salvador, their dialects sharpening my edge. Spanish? One of the few gold nuggets I pried from that mission muck.

So there I was, committed, boots planted, ready to roll. I'd studied my ass off, ready to preach deep, not parrot. If I was gonna preach what I'd been spoon-fed since diapers, I'd damn well get clear on it. Church says pray, you'll feel it, truth burning in your chest like a lit fuse. So I did, knees on the floor, sweat beading, scriptures open, praying over and over, "Show me, God, show me the truth," voice hoarse, night after night. Figured if you beg enough and no answer comes, you might trick yourself; believing is half the game. Could be a lucky penny glinting in the dirt, a cloud twisting into Jesus' beard, hell, anything'll do if you squint hard enough.

But no angel swooped down, wings blazing, whispering, "Joseph Smith's your prophet, kid." Cheers to those who get that Hollywood glow, gold plates and all, but not me. After the life I've lived, wild as it gets, at least for a Mormon boy, I can't help but wonder: maybe that forest floor in Palmyra, New York, where Joseph knelt, was laced with magic mushrooms. A nibble, a whiff of funky fumes, who knows? Takes me back to Boy Scouts, that Jamboree trip, hundreds of us tromping through the Sacred Grove in New York. No mushrooms I saw, but I wasn't hunting 'em. Did belt "Que Sera, Sera" with the crew inside the Statue of Liberty's hollow gut, all our squeaky puberty voices echoing off it's metal body, another badass perk Parker and the boys helped fund, tithing cash greasing the wheels for kids too broke to go.

Back to Uruguay, me and Rojas; no Joseph, no
Moroni, no Matthew, Mark, or miracles. Just us,
slogging it out. The clock ticked, slow as tar, and
I wanted it gone. I kept studying, pages flipping,
pencil scratching, hoping for clarity. It got worse
instead. The more I dug into the church's roots, its
fourteen year old girl polygamy tangles, gold plate
yarns, the less it held. Doubt crept in, a cold drip
down my spine. I prayed harder; no answers, just
silence. I felt used, a pawn in a white shirt. Still,
I racked up wins, high baptism numbers, dunking
souls in murky fonts. Not luck, I actually tried. I
cared about those Uruguayans, dirt-streaked kids,
moms with tired eyes, the ones breastfeeding in the
open, my favorite; I wanted their lives better, even
if my gospel pitch wobbled. Service mattered–
hauling water, fixing roofs–and that service stuck,
even as the faith frayed.

One hundred percent obedience was the mantra, a
relentless beat in the mission drumline. First year,
it was me to a T—6 a.m. alarm blaring through
humid dawn, studying 'til my eyes blurred, push-

ups on a creaky floor, sweat dripping, shower
under a lukewarm trickle, pray, scarf stale bread,
pray again, study more, proselyte 'til my throat
rasped. Lunch—a quick rice-and-beans break—
then back to knocking doors, serving, praying,
studying, preaching. Rinse, repeat—every damn
day, a treadmill of holy grind. Not once, pausing,
breath catching, staring at peeling walls, did I feel
closer to God. Tore through the Bible cover to
cover—ink smudged from my grip—reading to
know, not just check boxes. Footnotes scratched in
margins—"What's that mean?"—dictionary flipping back. Dug deep, no glossing over mysteries
like some drone chasing habits. Hit the Book of
Mormon again, Doctrine and Covenants too—
dog-eared, heavy in my hands—and no spark, no
burn. Could spit the script—Joseph Smith, prophet, golden plates, "Read, pray, God'll answer"—
smoother than anyone, voice like a salesman's. But
I was doubting, questions gnawing like termites
while I smiled through lessons.

Still, I carried on, one year down, sex with my
eternal companion dangling out there, a carrot
on a stick.I was good—bumped from peon grunt

knocking doors to district leader, then zone leader, barking orders, tallying baptisms. Never hit president's assistant—damn sure I was close, though. Elder Bankhead, Mission Prez, I liked—gray hair, steady eyes. He'd sit me down, office cluttered with papers, air thick with dust, and ask, "Elder, how do you feel in your heart?" Realest thing a suit ever said about the gospel—he cared, not about stats or font dunks, just what's inside. Most Christ-like slice of that mission, Bankhead's quiet care, making us feel seen. Sad twist: health tanked him early—unseen cracks—and he left. Died years later—heart attack, fifties, too young. God bless him and his family; he deserved better. Those heart-checks? It became clear I wasn't good—felt lied to, betrayed, a puppet strung by social pressure, preaching shit that didn't thrum in my chest. Heartbreaking, a slow shatter.

I hit a wall–couldn't do the perfect-slave act anymore. A year-plus in, my Spanish flowing, rules nailed–I was done. Time to go home, find what's me in my heart. I called Dad–I'm sure that was a surprise, no Mother's Day or Christmas chime, voice crackling over a shitty line. The living room faded as I spilled it: "I don't feel right, I wanna come home." Bishop Bob, deep in the church, heard me out, steady, calm. Don't recall it all, just the ache. Word spread fast. Parker and a posse of church bigwigs rang me up, voices booming. Same pre-mission bullshit: "You won't regret staying, the Lord will bless you," blah blah blah. Parker's call hit the hardest, I still had that flicker of marrying his daughter, her shy smile haunting me. But if she was all-in Mormon and my faith was fizzling like a wet sparkler, that old dream felt shaky. Those days, debating to stay or go, not one of 'em, not even Parker, asked, "What's in your heart?" Just pushed the line: "Toe it, reap the reward." That was it, the snap. I stopped giving a flying fuck. Heart sour, it flipped from bad to worse in a blink. Decided I'd stay, but no more leash. I'd live my way, rules be damned.

Mr. 100 Percent, overachiever king, kicked it to 200—a double life, slick as oil. Followed the script—taught, baptized, stats shining—while texting a girl on a smuggled phone, sneaking movies, popcorn crunching quiet. No one saw it—perk of being a machine; crank it higher, do more. Felt alive again—blood pumping—not a drone for the hive. Nice to live for me, not others. Truth? Didn't care—no one asked what I wanted. Tried bouncing honorably—suitcase half-packed—got hit with, "That'd be dishonorable." Shame, the kingdom's key: "Shame if you quit, shame if you can't hack two years." Celibate, pure, hadn't "sinned"—but to Uruguayan women—white tan skin, blue eyes—I was a catch: handsome American on a holy quest, damn near Jesus in khakis.

Didn't take long until I found a cute girl–sweet as hell, her smile like Parker's daughter, adjusted for a different shade of skin. That was it–her and me, fumbling, my first, hers too. Awkward, quick, a tangle of nerves on a sagging mattress, but it was done'd rejected girls before—holy water splashing, judging 'em low for "sin," sneering at ward gossip. Leaving that room—shame and a buzz humming—I got it, got Christ. He stood by the adulteress—"Where are thine accusers?"—dust settling as foes slunk off. All those I'd scorned, self-righteous prick that I was, and I understood now. Judgment, shame I'd heaped? Vanished. Just love, forgiveness, a pulse of grace. I found Christ in my "sin"--realized my real sin was that stone I'd clutched. No man's like Him if he spots flaws in others, none's clean to cast. That buzz? It grew the real Testicle King rising, a real son of the Almighty, born right there.

Stuck it out–damn near two years, 'til one month shy, when mono hit me like a truck. Uruguayan docs–fancy titles, shaky skills–misdiagnosed it as leukemia at first; it was a wild few days of blood tests and stale hospital air, my gut twisting 'til they sorted it. "Kissing disease," they call mono–ironic, right? Wondered if tongues wagged, but that one sweet kiss was ancient history, a year back, and not much sparked after. Tried keeping tabs–letters scrawled, stamps licked–but long-distance fizzles fast. That misdiagnosis scored me an early ticket home, plane engines humming, Montevideo shrank below, and I was thrilled, so fucking over that place, its dust, its grind. Landing back in America? Pure gold, wide roads, clean air, freedom hitting like a cold beverage after a desert slog. Best part? No more bunking with some tool who might be gay, snoring inches away, psychological abuse, straight up. My kids? Not a chance in hell they'll endure that shit, no MTC cage, no companion leash.

That double life my 200% game it worked like a charm. No one sniffed out my sidesteps– the texts, movies, that Uruguayan tumble–and I flew home, plotting my next move. I thought I'd track down Parker's daughter, her shy smile flickering in my head. But the shine was gone. That righteous Mormon life–perfect Molly Mormon wife in a crisp apron, church Sundays–soured fast. Could've buried it, taken it to my grave; you know plenty of Mormons do, right? Smiling in pews, temple cards flashing, all "soooo righteous" while hiding their own dirt. Seeing myself as one of those inauthentic fucks, grinning through gritted teeth, turned my stomach, bile rising at the thought. I came home anyway, did the rounds, gave my talks in packed chapels, voice steady: "Two years, Elder Walz, well done." Hands clapped my back, smiles beamed, praise raining like confetti. Inside? Done, cooked, plotting my exit while nodding through the bullshit, eyes on the door.

Chapter 4:

A New Heaven

That exit crashed in hard–excommunication, the church's scarlet letter. Spilled it all to a bishop, not my Dad, some BYU ward stiff in a cheap suit, office smelling of old carpet and guilt. Thought maybe it was my second chance, maybe I could repent, wipe the slate, go back to Mr. 100%; chalk that mission sin to a blip and lock it away. But that swirled with another plan, my real plan: Move on, get out, I can't fake this forever.

The process? A nightmare, God's an asshole if He designed it, but nah, just self-righteous pricks in ties cooked it up. Confession wasn't enough, I had to face a tribunal, stake president and his posse of twelve, a room of dickheads in a semicircle, ties straight, eyes cold. Wood-paneled walls closed in as they grilled me, "What positions? How many

times did you ejaculate? Describe every detail."
Stunned, jaw slack, I couldn't believe it. Who the
fuck were these guys? Never seen 'em in my life,
yet they're probing how I fucked that Uruguayan
girl, her breath, her skin, a moment they'd never
touch. Forgiveness? This was a goddamn inquisi-
tion, insanity, screaming *run*. I clammed up, gave
'em scraps, stared at the floor, scuffing my shoe
and they stamped me excommunicated. The mark
of shame: no sacrament, subtle public exile, bread
passing me by in church, heads turning.

Fallout hit fast, family arguments flared, voices
sharp over kitchen tables. "Move out," they said,
bags packed, door slamming behind me. Those
golden friends–pre-mission crew, paintball scars
and all–faded to distant nods, ghosts in the hall.
True colors bled out, Christ's "open arms" vanished, God's "worthy children" a hollow echo.
Didn't see it then, but my prayers were cracking
open, answered in the wreckage. Gotta say, God's
got a sick sense of humor, twisted, dark, perfect.
Love it, it's why I try to mirror it, that wry grin in
the chaos. Kicked out, but free, the Testicle King
stirred, crown tilting, ready to rise.

It wasn't all over—kindness glowed like cinders through the ash. Parker, ever the titan, funded my first gig: Splash Mobile Car Wash. Seed money from his deep pockets, a lifeline when I was raw from the church's boot. Mom, prude to the core—lips pursed, hands wringing—preached hard against it. "Risky," she'd hiss, "Parker's loan's debt, the devil's trap." Her voice dripped thrift-store guilt, but I shrugged it off, dove into sin, grabbed a credit card—plastic gleaming—and started living. Bounced around Provo in a beat-up Jeep, trailer in Tow, hose coiled, buckets sloshing—I built it from scratch. Brochures slick as hell, glossy under streetlights, my attention to detail a razor's edge, tires scrubbed 'til they shone, windows streaked free. That first hustle schooled me hard. Lesson one: you can't please every bastard. Some customers nitpicked—"Missed a spot," tires kicked, pushing 'til you'd give; others rolled easy, tipping with a grin. Life's split sharp: uptight pricks vs. lighthearted lovers, whether church pews, government halls, business deals, or bar stools. Gray's there, sure, but not much—assholes abound, fun folks shine. Park-er was the latter, my first client, rolling up in his truck, gravel crunching–kind but distant, a chill in his nod. Took his daughter out once, a post-mission date, her perfume soft, diner lights buzzing, but it fizzled. That old fantasy–righteous life, Molly Mormon bride–was a sham, dust in my mouth. I didn't want it anymore.

Even if I'd vibed with her, I'd morphed into such an overachiever, I couldn't stomach marrying the rich guy's daughter. Couldn't hack the whisper: "He hitched to Parker's cash." Me, the guy who'd impressed the titan, hustling, grinding, I didn't want it perceived that I'd cashed an easy ticket. Parker's world? Control freak central, no coffee maker in his RV, that Mormon steel unbent. Admired it–his jet-rich swagger, his rules–but I'd never slave to it, bowing under his thumb. I wanted to be him, not beholden to him.. Those mentors–Parker, Scott, Dee–were self-made kings who'd hauled themselves up from dirt. The idea that my success might look like a wedding-band shortcut? Not a chance. It tipped the scale hard. Even a glimmer with his daughter couldn't sway me; I craved my jet, my rags-to-riches epic, not a backstage pass to Parker's empire. Started dating wild–against

Mormon law– booze flowing, parties thumping. Beer in hand, cold and sweating, I'd laugh with the guys, bar stools creaking, or flirt with girls, neon buzzing overhead. Happy drunk—nothing nuts— occasional wild nights, shots clinking, but mostly a brew and a grin. My reset: a new dawn breaking, an entrepreneurial spark from kid days, hauling that red wagon, flickering back to life, burning hot in my chest.

I dated a slew of girls, post-mission whirl, hopping from one to the next. Even hooked up with Ben from the MTC's sister–my first real thing after Uruguay. She was wild, sexy as hell, all fire and curves, gym-obsessed, body proving it. Sparks flew, but like a lot of flings, it wasn't built to last, fizzling out in a haze of late nights and mismatched vibes. Her best line: "We just don't make sense anymore, let's just have sex, it's the only part that does." She was right, we were done, one last romp for the good times. Dozens of dates piled up–coffee shops, movie seats, small talk over fries– and my black-and-white theory clicked, especially with Mormon girls. It hardened into a principle I wield daily, a tool I call "sorting through bullshit." You see, just like those fake Mormons, smiling in church, temple cards flashing, hiding their dirt, there's two camps: the uptight masks and the ones like me, clawing to the core of who they are, what they want. This isn't just a life story for kicks–nah, I'm laying out the exact principle that rocketed me to success. This one's non-negotiable: life's short, moves fast–cutting to the bottom of shit quickly keeps the bullshit at bay.

Dating taught me early–girls sling semantics, pleasantries, nonsense like confetti. "Oh, how nice," "What's your major?", hours dribbling away on fluff. I wasn't playing games, I wanted real, wanted to move on. Freshly excommunicated, church's scarlet letter still hot on my chest, I need-ed a wife who wasn't some Molly Mormon fake bitch, all prim skirts and pious smirks. Dozens of dates–awkward silences, forced laughs–I wast-ed time on the usual chatter, but that didn't last. Slow-motion flirting–everyone else's pace–wasn't advancing me jack shit toward my goal. During my teen years, I'd devoured *The Millionaire*

Mind–stats on self-made kings, pages creased from late-night reads under a desk lamp. One standout? Marriage. Loads of those millionaires pegged their wins to a wife. Check the book for the nitty gritty, but the gist? Ditch the dating grind, lock in a teammate, split roles, and sprint to success faster. Ate that up; speedy success was my gospel. Sifting through girls at a crawl wouldn't cut it; I had to find my woman, sharp and swift.

So I flipped it–cut through bullshit by leading with my no-filter style on the first date. Picture it: me across a diner table, coffee cooling, neon buzzing, laying it out: "I'm excommunicated, fucked a girl on my mission, but I'm good–want someone who doesn't judge my past, values my blunt truth." Most recoiled, eyes widening, forks pausing, repulsed by raw honesty. Total transparency? A gut punch to folks comfy in their masks. But that's my tool: I don't want those people in my circle, not in business or in my personal life. If you flinch at bluntness, you're not my tribe. I want real, direct, flaws bared, no matter who you are. In Mormon land–Provo's sanctimonious sprawl–girls ghosted me fast, phones silent, no second calls. Win for me–sorting at warp speed–assholes out, lovers in. Took time, sure, but then Nichole–my match, that beautiful fucking angel–rolled into frame, no bull-shit, all fire.

Shit didn't unfold simply—twists hit hard. Parker had slipped Dad some front-row Jazz tickets at the Delta Center–sweet deal, twelve primo spots. Bossman was supposedly out of town, shilling them to Dad like he often did, a casual handoff. Dad tossed 'em my way, but wires crossed. Parker wasn't gone, he'd be there too. I didn't know that, just rolled with it, holder in due course of a stack of tickets, Jeep Grand Cherokee purring, upgraded from my old Wrangler. My buddy Dave rode shot-gun, grinning–we cruised Freedom Boulevard–hunting chicks, my regular gig. Hitting on girls was cake–you spot 'em, talk, done. Easier with bait like courtside seats, dangling that hook snagged 'em fast. We pulled alongside a little Chevy Co-balt at a stoplight, engine humming, three girls inside. Couldn't see into the back seat–tiny, tinted window–but there was Nichole, my future wife, heart-thumping love at first sight. I leaned out, hollering to her sister and friend: "Got front-row tickets to tomorrow's game, any takers?" Not my usual types, but I wasn't picky, just filling seats: four up front, eight a few rows back, group-date vibe, whoever wanted in.

The front girls hesitated–eyes darting, lips pursed– but a voice piped up from the back, cool and sure: "Give him my number." Nichole–not a party girl– was tagging along with her sister and friend, head- ed to some low-key hangout, fresh off a Mormon breakup, her high school boyfriend swallowed by the mission grind. But through that tiny window, she saw me, and marked me as hers. Took her digits in my newly acquired Iphone, light turned green, and we peeled off. Met her later–the local pool hall–she was stunning, hot blonde, small town vibe.. I mapped out the game plan: pick 'em up, haul ass to Salt Lake. Curveball–another girl I'd hit up, casual friend, no big romance, had flaked, but then flipped available last-minute. I figured, why not? She'd roll too. Loaded the crew, Nich- ole, her sister, the friend, Dave–into the Jeep, tires humming up I-15, Delta Center lights glowing. In my head, it's a blast; get to know Nichole, cute and new, but group-style, low stakes. Always aimed to keep folks happy, so I'd sit with her and the friend–it was a chill plan. Then the universe chucked a wrench.

Walked in, court buzzing, sneakers squeaking, and there's Parker, his daughter beside him, striding across right next to my seats. Dad swore Parker was out, traveling. Setup? Were Dad and Parker scheming? A casual "accident" to nudge us together? No clue, mind spinning. No small fry: those tickets were Parker's gift, kindness I couldn't spit on. But I'm rolling in with two dates–Nichole and the friend–and now his daughter's in the mix, expectations murky as hell. Sat down, sweat prickling–Parker's daughter on my left, prim in her sweater–Nichole on my right, new and sparking. Figured I'd play it safe. Halftime switch: swapped Nichole for the friend, sent my future wife a few rows back with Dave, her sister, the crew. Parker's daughter stayed on my left–quiet, unreadable, casual friend on my right, chatting easy. Old life flashed–front-row forever, Mormon dream tempting me back–comfy but fake. It was an overwhelming pickle, caught between worlds, seats creaking under me.

Game ended, buzzer blaring, we thanked Parker, his nod cool, and rolled out with my gang of twelve. Hit the Hard Rock Cafe downtown. Practiced my bluntness there, pulled Nichole aside, looking straight into her beautiful blue eyes, beer in my hand, and laid it out: "Sorry for the shuffle, I didn't know Parker'd be here, didn't wanna disrespect his seats, thought he might expect me with his girl." Full story, honest, no filter. Fun night, sure, crowd roaring, but Nichole passed the test: three girls in orbit, my chaos on display, and she didn't flinch. Dropped 'em off, Jeep rumbling back to Provo, and that was that. The test continued, though; high-intensity Ryan energy unleashed: life story dumped, "Here's me, take it or leave it," blunt as a sledge. She still picked up, beautiful voice warm: "Your honesty's refreshing." Later, I'd learn it wasn't *all* refreshing all the time–more on that later. But I get it. Sixteen years hitched now, Nichole and me. No marriage is perfect, it's a fucking hard grind through shitstorms sometimes. But we're here, shining, still slicing through bullshit when we clash. Three months after meeting, December snow falling, we were engaged. By that next April–rings swapped and vows sealed.

It wasn't smooth sailing, not even close. Nichole and Ryan's start wasn't just a beginning; it kicked off a damn avalanche. She rolled with my bluntness, eyes sparking when I'd cut through the noise, but her family? They gagged on it. She still laughs about my first visit to their place–countryside cabin, lawn tight, air thick with potpourri. I strode in, boots scuffing their hardwood, and laid it out: I ditched BYU 'cause school's a churn for drones, and those grads'd punch clocks for me someday. Confident, brash, me being me. Nichole smirked, then whispered later over dish clatter, "Maybe tone that down around them."

Saga launched: a wife split two ways from day one, her new life with me crashing against her old one. She craves the freedom I bring–blunt honesty, no masks–but her family's judgment creeps in like damp rot. Torn between worlds, it's heartbreaking, rips her up inside. Me? I don't bend for the unpleasable–seen it gut you slow, wreckage firsthand. Her pleas to soften up for them? Deaf ears–I'd vowed to be me, take it or leave it. Her folks didn't love it–bet they figured we'd fizzle quick, Nichole rebounding to that missionary boy when he rolled back, tie still knotted. God–or Ryan–had other blueprints.

Within a year, Nichole was pregnant–baby number one, a curveball to the gut. News dropped like a brick through glass–her family didn't cheer; they fractured. Her mom, tears trembling, didn't gush joy, just wailed: "This isn't what you wanted, Nichole, you were gonna go to school, do so much more." Overwhelmed, like a pregnancy was a derailment, not a dawn. Crushed me, our spark of us met with gloom. Called her mom, my voice steady: "Crying won't change it lady, she's pregnant, we're having this baby. Abortion's not us; it's done." No point arguing facts, belly growing, life kicking. Nichole? Devastated, eyes red, hands clutching mine, our joy dimmed by that sting. Then Bob—Dad, the rock–flipped the script fast. That man's never missed a beat, every win, big or small, gets his grin, warm as a hearth, and a celebration to match. Tradition kicked in: every pregnancy, we'd pile into his truck, leather seats creaking and hit Park City, this little Mexican joint tucked off Main,

Bob toasting us, glass raised, pride beaming. It's one of those gems Nichole and I'll clutch forever, taco grease on our fingers, laughter bouncing off adobe walls. Bob's not just my father—he's Nichole's too.

My method–cutting through the bullshit like a blade through fog–works, slices clean, but damn, it's got teeth, consequences that bite back. I should've vetted Nichole's family too, run 'em through the same test. Hindsight's 20/20, crystal now, blurry then, and in the end, they don't matter. It's her, me, our life–that's the core, the beating heart. Ryan's rules are simple: set the goal, chase it hard, and anyone who can't pass the test–family or not–gets left on the curb. Success demands it–a tough pill. Systems–religions with their steeples, governments with their suits, even families, cling to old ways, tangled in stubbornness like roots in rocky soil. They can't let go, can't see past the script. Sometimes you've gotta ditch 'em–loved ones too–not out of hate, not forever if you're lucky; but their creaky traditions can't derail who you're meant to be. True family, like Bob, comes around. They'll see it eventually: you're chasing your heart. My favorite gut-check I ask myself in the quiet hum of night: *What's in your heart?* Old lives muddle it, past clashing with present, and you've got to pick: grip the ghost of what was or grow into what's blooming.

There's this book–*Full Catastrophe Living*–title nails it. Beat-up copy on my shelf, pages creased from late reads. Sometimes, for the new dream to spark, the old one's gotta burn out, ashes scattering in the wind. Life's truth? Change is the only constant, a river carving stone. Cling to the past, and it slips anyway, fingers grasping air. My methods demand old ways pass, gentle or brutal, no other path. Those clutching yesterday? Age and death win; nature's trick to clear the board for new blood, new ideas. I've never been one to chain the past to now– I'm always forging fresh, sparks flying. Nichole wants it too, freedom humming in her veins; but she's torn, split raw. Her sister's even said it, voice sharp over coffee steam: "Wish my husband knew the *old* Nichole." Part of her might itch to dust off that ghost like an old photo, but I'd bet my boots she'd rather her sister love the new her–bold, unshackled. Judgment and shame–same

shit I slogged through in the Mormon maze–get
weaponized against change, guilt slung like mud.
But here's the kicker: fight it, and change rolls *anyway*, bigger, louder, a goddamn explosion if you
resist it. I've learned to roll with it–next rule up.

When you sort the bullshit, chasing your future
self–goals sharp as a blade–it stirs shit up. Chaos
brews, rages flare, family glares with voices raised,
old ties snapping like dry twigs. You know the saying, "This too shall pass"? Let it. Rage roars like
a storm wind, chaos swirls like a dust devil. Step
aside, let it blow through. Fighting it's a mess–fists
clenched, gut knotted–but peel yourself free, and
it's just noise that's not yours to carry. Struggle?
Rage? Chaos? It rules you if you resist it, frees you
when you don't. When you shrug off the mess,
it's an easier ride to where you're headed, dreams
gleaming ahead. Full catastrophe living–embrace
the crash, watch it fade, and keep moving.

Becoming a father flips you inside out. Seeing a
tiny human with your spark in his eyes, forged
from her and me. Weird as hell, visceral, messy,
but a miracle, nature's raw pulse, the circle of life

spinning on. Game time hit, I locked in, just like *The Millionaire Mind* preached: find a queen,, build the team, and win fast. I had her, the best her–Nichole–not just any wife. She's sharp, sexy– beautiful eyes glinting like dawn, charm bubbling over, full of life and love, hungry for the world through my lens–not just open but ravenous for it. The desire for freedom burns in her, bright, fierce– but she's a Mormon girl, raised in shame's thick fog. She's hacked through the weeds of old ways, staggering, chest heaving. Growing up in that church, Nichole, like so many young women, got fed the infamous rose lesson: passed hand-to-hand in a sterile classroom, petals soft at first, beauty pristine. By the last girl, the rose is crushed–a sad, fucked-up analogy for her sexuality. Message drilled: get touched, you're used–worth fades, a dead flower. Psychological wreckage? Unfathomable. Therapists bankrolled it, grinning as the checks rolled in.

Even as her first, sex is wild between us–amazing, but that rose rots in her head, dragging her down. Mormon youth classes jammed it in: pure 'til you're not, then you're spoiled, wilted. Even married, she'd wrestle it–eyes dimming some nights, thinking "a m I still that flower?" Breaks my heart–that poison's a lie from Sunday School. I'd torch it from every pulpit, and sear into my daughters' souls their God-given worth–no matter who they've slept with or what checkered past trails behind. Church always preached: "Young men, don't objectify women", voices booming from podiums, yet in those classrooms, they turned girls into objects, roses to be ruined, value crumbling with a touch. Jesus stood by the adulteress, saying, "Neither do I condemn thee," so how the hell do these "teachers of Christ" peddle that rose garbage? Hypocrisy thick enough to choke on.

Baby number two rolled in just eighteen months later, another beautiful boy, chubby cheeks and wide eyes. Less family chaos this time, muted grumbles instead of wails, but still no easy glide you'd hope for. From marriage to our second kid, I locked in–Millionaire Mind humming–Nichole on my team, world's best wife, radiant, charm like a live wire. I dove into the grind. Tea Party Tee, Kivia (my MLM crack), car washing, odd jobs–I hustled it for every gig. Struggled hard–crashed in my parents' basement, concrete walls closing in, air stale with laundry and tension. Nichole and I bickered, who wouldn't? Living with in-laws is a pressure cooker–works, but rough as hell, tempers flaring over dishes. She'd push for a house, voice sharp, eyes pleading–I'd refuse, jaw set. The system didn't want us free. Slave route? Punch a clock for three months–bam, house loan approved, keys jingling. Business owner? Three years of profit on paper before a bank blinks. Fuck that–that rigged fuckery lit my fire. Wrong's wrong: men and women building businesses–pouring sweat, guts, soul– deserve homes as much as any cubicle drone. First few years, that was the hot coal, grief from her family, "You need a house," their voices dripping pity. What the fuck were they gonna do about it? Shovel cash? Nah, just whine. When Nichole's sister moved in with her folks to save, praise heaped, no shade. Me? "Ryan's gotta provide, what's he doing?"--nasal bullshit I don't swallow.

Nichole's split–her new life with me, old life with them–cracked wider, a chasm of judgment. I was hellbent that one business would pop; I knew it, gut-deep. Freedom was the prize–mentors like

Parker, Scott, Dee, book authors, mapped the path: grind, then break free. Early years were brutal, scraping by, coins clinking. Thank God for Parker–he waived the last chunk of my car wash loan as a wedding present, a lifeline when we were drowning. That kindness? Pure him–quiet moves, no spotlight, too many stories of his grace he'd rather keep hushed–checks slipped to the broke, doors opened for the down. Why I chased wealth–money is power, energy pulsing. Time's great, sure, but mix it with cash? Unbeatable leverage, every move amplified. Parker's generosity to others stoked my goal: money was also unlimited juice to reach, to give, when the world kicks someone low.

Baby two shifted gears. Parents' basement, damp and tight, wasn't cutting it. Reinvesting every dime into my hustles, skipping rent, food stretched thin, couldn't hold much longer. Second son squalling fresh, I grabbed a "normal" job–soul-crushing, clock in, clock out, a cog in the machine–felt like I'd caved, dream gutted. If I'd known then what I know now, I'd have seen it was the spark about to ignite.

I started managing Parkway Storage Center in Orem, metal units gleaming under Utah sun, gravel crunching underfoot. Like every gig, I turned it, used the paycheck to grow, sustain, keep the wheel spinning. Invested every scrap, tithing to my future, a principle I'd later bake into my Saints of the Future church. No ten percent to steeples here; pay it to yourself. Every month, no excuses, grab at least ten percent of your haul and shove it into stocks, crypto, assets, your own hustle. Got a business? Bank it for the next. Tithing's faith in tomorrow, seeds sown. Reap that harvest, and you're perched to lift others, the fruit of your grind. Self-faith is God-faith–He'll juice your yield to help the fallen. I gave that job everything, eyes sharp, every detail a chance. Didn't know how it'd pay off, just knew it would–God, Universe, drawing me to soar.

I'm an observer–facts, details, people's ticks–and when systems stomp the downed, it churns my gut. Storage gig? Standard play: evict tenants who miss rent–can't pay, can't stay. Fair enough, 'til you see the rest. Can't pay? We auction your stuff, boxes ripped open, lives sold cheap–and if it doesn't cover the tab, collections hunt you down.

Beating on a beating, kicked while bleeding. Most tenants? Jobless, rent late, scrambling–now their last scraps, shit they could've sold to survive, locked tight, held hostage 'til the storage gods got their cut. Auctions rolled, balances lingered, sent to the hounds. Made me sick, I couldn't stand it. Owners? Decent guys, kind, sure, but drones to the game, trained by other facilities, lawyers shrugging: "That's how it's done." Their grace? They let me flip it, my way. Boom, the opportunity cracked open: prove business success doesn't have to feast on the little guy's bones. My shot to test an ideology–freedom, not fuckery.

At Parkway Storage, I was buzzing–feeling good, a machine humming on all cylinders. Side hustles piled up, stocks ticking on my phone, random gear flipped on classifieds, houses gutted and polished– name it, I was in it. No loss to the storage gig either–revenue climbed, $100k up in one year, numbers glowing like a scoreboard. That taught me that 100k in new revenue can add 1.6 million in value to the business. Proved I'm a fucking beast–boss couldn't blink at that resume. Time to stop earning for others, time for me.

Pitched my original mentor, Boss Man Parker–the titan, king–if he'd jump into storage with me. Crushed me when he said no, I dreamed of empire-building side-by-side, penthouse views over the city. His response hit me hard: "I appreciate your pitch, Ryan, you might wanna partner with me, but I've gotta wanna partner with you." Gut punch, lesson landed: can't force a deal with someone who's not in. Kept pitching him over the years–ego bruised but stubborn as hell–and was met with, "Admire your grit, but…" Eventually, I quit–not cause I quit on me–but bullshit cuts both ways. Clinging to that childhood Mormon fantasy, Parker as my golden ticket, was a ghost I'd nursed too long. Fire still burned; I didn't need him.

New player stepped up–Richard–eyes widening at my Parkway track record, dollar signs flashing. Dilemma? He wasn't a 50/50 guy, had a control freak streak- he'd renegotiate deals after they were agreed to and tout it at as "good business," I call it fuckery. I didn't care I had a hook: 66% for Richard and 33% of new value for me on a storage unit deal. If he dropped $3 million to buy and we sold for $6 million, I'd snag 33% of the $3 million gain—$990,000. Plus, juice up yearly profit from $100k to $200k? Another $33k or more a year on my base pay. Huge upgrade, side gigs still humming, level-up locked. I scoured the market, dozens of facilities, spreadsheets sprawling, growth stats crunched. Offers flung, none stuck. Had cash, a deal to shift my life, and nothing landed 'til my birthday. Herriman Storage, in Herriman, Utah, closed on my twenty-seventh birthday, ink drying as cake candles flickered. Seminary days as a Mormon kid, the teacher had us scribble our futures. Mine? Clear as day: millionaire by 30, billionaire by 40. Jet money, baby. Stock wins, flips, side gigs, now this, I was rolling, three years to that first million, a lock.

Nichole and I squatted in flip houses–drywall dust, paint fumes–tastes of the dream. Profits piled, and I'd growl over takeout: "We'll buy our own house in cash, fuck the banks, fuck the bullshit." Told her we'd do it differently, others snag houses now, drown in double interest. Us? Wait, believe, strike free. Brutal on her–eyes tired some nights, faith stretched thin–but she stuck by me, not always thrilled, days she'd rather bolt. Though split still–

old ways tugging, new ways calling–she'd grit her teeth and pick the new, every time. Trooper–the toughest wife, best mom–couldn't dream better. Finally, moved from flip chaos and Mom's basement to Herriman's caretaker unit–no more in-law thermostat wars–fresh air, Herriman buzzing up-and-coming. Empire's first notch carved–game on.

Like Parkway, I flipped the script. No collections agencies; fuck that noise. Old manager's computer porn? Wiped, screen clean. Office deep-cleaned, bleach sharp, floors gleaming. Year one? Another $100k bump, limits hit eventually–can't juice forever without losing tenants–but I crushed it. Bought at $3 million, sold later for nearly $7 million, more on that down the road. Two boys in tow, third brewing–partners Richard and crew grinned at monthly draw checks, profits swelling every six months to a year. They didn't know my full heat– Richard's dumb moves later proved it–but God slung me miracles, wild ones.

Chapter 5:

Boats and Tows

A year in, Herriman humming, I itched to grow. American Fork, Utah deal popped, raw land, boat storage potential. Grinding the numbers, dirt under my nails, spreadsheets late-night glowing– the partnership offered on it was murky. The guy pitching forgot a detail: foreclosure loomed, him bailing after a hell-run. Development's brutal, that red tape strangling, hoops absurd, winners are superheroes dodging bullshit fees and studies. Trump gets it, hardcore. To me: Dubai's proof: sand dunes to sci-fi skyline in thirty years, no Jetsons saucers, but damn close. The U.S.? Stalled, Elon's D.O.G.E. exposes why: political fraud, fees over progress, greedy fucks pocketing cash. American Fork guy lost it to the crooked bank; my heart ached for him. Fight 'em? Maybe he did, maybe not, gone either way. The bank sniffed our interest and offered it up. This time, I roped Dad in–Bob, Richard, me, Richard's dead brother's family via trustee. His brother was an early investor who passed not long after we partnered. I liked him better than Richard based on our phone chats– warmer vibe, less shark. Bob tossed in a few hundred grand, partners matched, bank loaned the rest, same bank that foreclosed. The empire swelled, sixteen acres richer, raking it in.

When we flipped houses, I was all in–I hired help, sure, but I also swung the hammer. Not a single task I can't tackle: framing studs, plumbing pipes, electric, drywall, paint– whatever, I'd do it, done it. My life's motto–dive in, figure it out, sometimes lands me in shit, but mostly it's a blast, lessons burning deep. Game time hit again: 16 acres next to a boat harbor–Boat and RV Storage. If I could pull this off, I could conquer anything. Clueless what I was stepping into–Russian olive trees clawing the dirt, saving one acre with curb, gutter, and storm drain from the last guy, but I knew I'd crack it. Old owner's plans got us started but the stingy bank wouldn't share, so we paid fresh, redrew everything. Tweaked it hard: no dinky units, big warehouses, full service. Drop your boat after a lake day–sunburned, wind-whipped–we'd wash it, fuel it, tuck it away, ready when you roll back. Name brainstormed over a conference call landed on Marina Cove Storage. Perfect, I was pumped. One hitch: no building without a permit, no permit without a commercial license. Enter my father-in-law, he had the creds, small town contractor. My gut churned–work with him? Him with me? Torture both ways–but profit lured us in. To his credit, he bit–he's no dummy–and we teamed up. Went decent, at least 'til the cracks began to show.

First hurdle: excavation, hundreds of Russian olives choking the land. Loved it–me and him snagged a backhoe, engine growling, and for months I plowed through mud–thorns snapping, books on tape blaring in my ears: Abraham Hicks, Wayne Dyer, Joe Dispenza, Neville Goddard. New voices, wild ideas, same core: laws of the universe, law of attraction. Believe it, you'll see it: thoughts and feelings shape reality. I soaked it in like a dry canyon gulch. Focus on what you want, feel it, and the universe delivers, anything? Really, anything? Yet it matched my life–I'd scribbled "millionaire by 30" as a kid, and here I was, past that, not even 30 yet. Dreams manifested, hard to argue, but I wasn't totally convinced. After all, I did this–I raised rents, axed collections, built the wins. Me, not some cosmic vibe. My own cognitive dissonance, old foe from Mormon days, reared up, internal now. Boy, did it wrestle inside me.

Those books–tapes spinning as olives flattened–pitched a mindfuck: chill out, hit a beach, let it flow. Me? The overachiever—200% always, never 100, letting go felt like betrayal. "Let God"? Rough–my brain twisted, looking at the dirt caking my boots. But I was learning fast: one man can't do it all. Running that backhoe, dreaming an empire–office help, sometimes even Nichole pitching in to run things–kept Herriman humming. She's an introvert–strangers at the desk drained her, voice tight helping tenants–but she'd step up, keys jingling when we were strapped. I was stretched thin, spreadsheets glowing late, bathrooms scrubbed, units swept, lawns mowed, paint slapped, snow plowed–did it all, good too. Another facility to bring to life–boat washing, oil changes, a whole new beast. Law of attraction idea crept in slowly–took a year–but it stuck. The new office rose, shiny caretaker's unit upstairs, 40 big units gleaming below. Phase 1–we moved in–and our first baby girl was born, kid number three. Nichole and I? When it's good, it's good–baby-making magic.

Hired a full-time manager for Herriman–a gut punch–losing some of my salary to pay her. Proof I couldn't solo it, the law of attraction sharpened: empires need hands–you can't hoard the cash. I never paid cheap. Richard's voice sometimes taunted, "Renegotiate, skim more,"--an evil whisper, the devil's nudge. I fought it, I gave big to my help, always, even when it stung. Phase 1 proved it–20,000 square feet, rents rolled, value spiked. Phase 2–30,000 square feet, built on sweat equity, my labor, my time. No extra partner cash–and the units filled fast. Phase 3? Big warehouse, 30,000 sq. ft.--more units, lake shore gold. The catch? 100-year floodplain–water could climb 8 feet above most of our land every century. Had to raise it–8 feet of fill dirt across 12 acres. Dirt's cheap, right? Wrong, moving it's a beast: loaders groaning, dump trucks rumbling, fuel guzzling, hours bleeding. $2 million in excavation. Sweet Jesus, dreams of low-cost builds evaporated–a new mess, no collections agents or attorneys to curse. Just me, begging dirt, law of attraction staring me down.

We were stuck, equity stacked from sweat, Phase 3 primed–but I couldn't build without dirt. Fuck-tons of it, engineered fill was pricey as hell, for the foundations and floors. No dodging it–20, sometimes 50 loads a day rolling in, dust swirl-ing–10-12 inches spread, compacted tight, backhoe rumbling, soaking it, checking it, layering again. Dirt nearby was gold, but go far and costs spike: miles, hours, fuel guzzling. Problem? Clean dirt's scarce and landfill trash won't cut it. We ran dry– some guy digging house foundations hauled loads 'til he tapped out–leaving us feet shy, tons of feet. Every day, interest ticked, and millions in loans bleeding me dry. I used to think $60k a year was solid; now I was hemorrhaging that on interest alone monthly–it was wild, daunting, but I was in. No risk, no reward.

Then those law of attraction voices, Hicks, Dyer, Dispenza, started echoing. I noticed a trend: fixate on "no dirt," and no dirt showed. Coincidence? Maybe, or maybe this manifesting shit was real. It was my time to test it– stuck, desperate, why not?, what could I lose? I stopped saying "no dirt" (cringes me now, you say it, you get it). I took Nichole to Vegas, my playground, neon buzzing, slots chiming. Convinced her for a hot minute to swing, wild nights, drinks flowing, but it flopped fast. Drunk Nichole? Party gold, loose, laughing, no nudge needed, but sober? Walls up, baggage heavy. And things we did drunk, my fault? Hindsight: don't drunk-dive where sober you won't swim–liquid courage can fuck you sideways.

Set dirt aside, hit Vegas, aimed to feel it solved. The dirt will show up–hell, it's already there. No fretting, no hunting, law of attraction on trial. Post Vegas weekend–still buzzing from blackjack, sex, and sun–shiny dump trucks rolled up, dirt spilling, not one call made. Magic? Maybe. I turned it into a game–unload, compact, wait. Nothing–no calls, no deliveries–out of dirt again. So we'd bolt to Vegas, Arizona, sunshine blazing, the idea: get happy, let go. Every damn time, dirt showed, trucks growling, piles rising. Stay and scramble for sources?

Crickets, no fucking dirt. Clearest proof yet–go, have fun, let God. Jesus' words rang, childhood echoes: "Whatsoever ye shall ask, believing, ye shall receive." Were they right, just words mangled by Morons (Mormons)? The more I live, the more I'm sold–organized religion's the Devil's smoke– truth's in the hearts of men, not pews, no big build- ings or malls required.   John 4:24; "When the true worshipers will worship the Father in spirit and truth," Matthew 18: 20; "For where two or three are gathered in my name, there am I among them."

.

Phase 3 crawled–90,000 square feet–not solo, lots of subcontractors–lifelines I'm damn grateful for. Empire is co-creation–you can't do it alone. Cash got tight–redirected Phase 1 and 2 rents to interest, borrowed heavily. Once–$80k short on an invoice–my gut sinking, no clue where to pull it. Then it clicked, "Dirt showed up; money will too." Weeks of stress, then I let go: "I can't, but God can." Next day, banker rings, voice crack- ling: "Ryan, we fucked up, missed $80k on your construction loan drop. Wired it today, sorry for the mix-up." I couldn't fucking believe it, voodoo on bankers, manifesting magic, wild as hell. The Universe coughed up $80k and the sub got paid, my jaw dropped. Just one story but shit gets crazier, so buckle up. The Law of attraction's real, start practicing.

Red tape bullshit flared, American Fork's building manager–a stingy, self-serving prick–warred with us. Neighbors, architects, nobody had a kind word; their tales biased me hard. Thrive on misery? Hell's got a spot for you. But it clashed with my positivity push; Wayne Dyer's tale of forgiving a foe with flowers stuck. Six months to a year post-Phase 3–still no occupancy permit. This fucker and his lackeys nitpicked endlessly: "Need an 'End of Path' sign", bike path to nowhere we'd donated, "Add a firewall", on steel units, drywall atop steel–absurd. Common sense? Fine, maybe some requests I'd stomach, but re-inspection's dragged, days to weeks, holidays stalling, months bleeding, empty buildings, loan interest ticking. No temporary permit, no mercy, "A Fire hydrant in Phase 4," they'd say. Phase 4? What the fuck? We were building phase 3. Insanity piled.

Chapter 6:

For the Nuts

Testicuzzi, born at Lake Powell, sister-in-law's "ball-cuzzi"--a tale of red cups, bubbles, my threesome sexy vibe, lit me up. A hot tub for your nuts, no joke, why not? I had a lifetime of entrepreneur dreams, like cosmic ping pong, robotic chess, notebooks of Testicle King gold, waiting. Investors balk at unproven–good luck pitching a nuts-soaker prospectus. Real estate funded my risks–storage, stocks–cash flowed, and Testicuzzi? Viral, millions in sales, hundreds of millions of views, marketing fees near zero. A Gold mine, fun, sexy, creative, and me shit-test filtering tight-asses over the whole world. New ideas were being born, but I was stuck on Marina Cove. I needed occupancy.

Wayne Dyer's forgiveness hit again. Wayne, you fucking genius. I sent a gift basket to the city's building department–my Testicuzzi front and center–(yep, Testicle King rising), bath bombs nestled, two to represent balls, and a note scrawled: "Sorry for busting your balls, designed this for the pain. Hope it helps – Ryan." The very next day an occupancy permit was taped to the door. The law of attraction is fucking real–my problems, well, those are on me.

It was wilder than I'd pictured, those Marina Cove units filled fast, cash rolling in like a tide. We needed it, catching up from lean years, but we were doing it, damn it. Herriman hummed smooth, manager crushing it. I tackled Marina Cove daily, and now Testicuzzi. Who'd have thunk a hot tub for your balls, not some Jacuzzi knockoff, would hit? Jacuzzi sent a cease-and-desist—paper crisp, lawyers snarling, claiming we might muddle their brand. Three attorneys I spoke to shrugged: "Cut losses, run." Fuck that, I don't fold. I found a pitbull lawyer who'd bite back; Jacuzzi blinked, a multibillion-dollar giant vs. our gag gift, not worth their court time. Nor mine–but I wasn't quitting. Wasn't riding their coattails by any stretch; Testicuzzi was mine, a riff off "Beer Cuzzi," balls in a cup, funny as hell, no overlap with their spa empire. Glad it died there, though a lawsuit's buzz might've blown us to billions. Influencers latched on, viral clowns riding our wave, some got famous just dunking their nuts on camera. Woke up one morning–coffee still hot–to $100k in sales overnight. One night. A testicle-fucking hot tub, unbelievable. But I'd manifested it, believed in it, felt it, and bam, there it was.

Testicuzzi wasn't all champagne; problems piled like wet towels. Production? Thought it'd be fast, cheap, simple vibrating ball-bubbler. Nope, red tape strangling: shipping snarls, inspections dragging, revisions chewing time. Crash course in making shit it still humbles me. Makes me kiss the iPhone, components clicking perfect, delivered slick an engineering wet dream. Testicuzzi birthed the Testicle King, me, Ryan, forged in excommunication fires, family shame, all the bullshit you've read. Honed my sift-fast rule, cut through the crap, and Testicuzzi turbocharged it. Our tagline? "For the nuts"—us, the wild, nutty, creative fringe. Beyond ball-bubblers, we slung hats, tees, favorite's "Hap-Penis," my Uncle Pride's genius plug, joy's cheeky wink. Rock that hat with Pride (pun intended), bullshit filter on blast. Mormon Karen's snarl, barking commentary; but magic happens with the rest: "Cool hat, man!" "That's hilarious!" Gray zoners smirk, half-convinced, teetering. The world's black-and-white dominates, gray's the safe perch, folks scared to pick. Black sheep like me, fringe, leading edge, Abraham Hicks' vibe. White sheep cling, I shove: "Drop the old, come on in!" They lean eventually, it's nature's pull, my Hap-Penis hat a nudge for some. Shit-testing made easy, right there on my forehead.

We're all waking, souls, timing it right. I hope my irreverence, cocky, loud, sways a few, this book sparking some backhoe dreamer like those tapes did me. It's magic, life's breath, fires forging us, journey's pulse. I'm the black sheep–the creative soul, torch lit, burning the world down, stacking bills. My mentors taught me, and if I did it, you fucking can. Party's open–wealth, freedom–for anyone who'll grab it.

Back when I was holed up in Bob and Michelle's basement, newborn wailing, I'd take the late-night shift rocking my son while the TV flickered. Loved those late-night shows, screen flashing WARN-ING, WARNING, a neon buzz cutting through the haze. What an era–sex-drenched commercials hawking hotlines, sandwiched around a gem I'd tune in for: Art Mann Presents. Some of you know it–a wild ride every time. Art would crisscross the USA, chasing drunken chaos, epic parties, reckless adventures, boobs flashing free. I fucking loved it; it was a perfect wind-down after a brutal day, baby snoozing on my chest. Brought me joy, raw and unfiltered; it must've etched something deep. Art got the bullshit test, diving into the world's underbelly–places Mormons wouldn't touch with a 100-foot pole, too steeped in shame, too "filthy." But down there, it's alive, pulsing. DNA tests spill it now: whoopsie nights, affairs, rape, mo-lestation, incest, way more common than polite society whispers. I'm not advocating rape and the like–fuck no–just cracking the taboo open, shin-ing a flashlight on the dark. Nichole and I dipped into swinging, an ironic twist; it's actually more rampant in Mormon Utah than prudes admit. BYU dorms? Docking, dry humping, backdoor action, everything but the "sinful" plunge–justified 'cause everyone does it and no one says it.

Art Mann, to me, was a courage king, bridging the gap between fake and real. Nichole leaps daily to stay hitched to me while clutching her family ties. Sad truth? That chasm's widened– partly my fault, I'll own it. In a black-and-white world, us black-team renegades push buttons hard. Art's show was unvarnished, and the chaos didn't scare me off. Showed life's messy side that Mormons and religious types bury, pretending it's not there. That denial? It births guys like me, Hap-Penis hat blazing, carving a haven for the shoved-in-the -closet parts folks hide. Plenty do; shame's a heavy lock. Post-Testicuzzi launch, sales spiking, my childhood late-night hero, Art Mann, rang me up. He loved it, right up his alley–how could he not? He's a natural-born shit-tester, soul-wired to shred the matrix, wake the sleepers. And my nut-soaker? A shit-test incarnate, and the king of late-night TV shit-testing's on the line.

Didn't take long, Art and I clicked. We were cut from the same cosmic cloth, flung into the world as cure or curse–but damn sure to have some fucking fun. Two black sheep, laughing loud, ready to burn it all down. That first call with Art Mann sparked the Testicle Empire, our YouTube series–nothing wild, just a side hustle for kicks. Chasing YouTube stardom, a whack at fun–we're still grinding it–and like everything I touch, I won't quit. My Testicle Empire notebook's ballooned, ideas spilling past my other invention scribbles, but big shit brewing.

I've dabbled in it all–shrooms melting reality, ecstasy buzzing electric, molly softening edges, cocaine sharp as a blade, weed hazing the room. Sexually? Swinging days opened doors, couple swaps, threesomes, experimental tangles. Loved a lot of it–Nichole, some of it, and we scored some real-as-hell friends. Underbelly folks? Rawest you'll meet, no suits, no shtick, just naked truth. Mormons? Shame locks 'em up, and secrets fester. But swinging, stripped bare, there's literally nothing hidden. Booze flowing, truth spills, judgment fades 'til sobriety snaps it back. Partying felt like home– people screwing up, owning it, no masks. Secretly, everyone's dipped–drunk chats, sober ones too–real as fuck. Sloppy tales, bare skin, just chilling, no stakes, no judgment. That's the life I crave. Testicuzzi's my flag, not just a gag, a beacon for shit-test passers, bold souls flipping off the old guard.

Chapter 7:

The Nanny

Nichole and I tried it all, awkward as hell sometimes, shit we'd never whisper. She's phased out, locked down, done opening up. That wild side–sex, parties, realness–fuels me, and the Testicle Empire's my window back. Mistakes? Plenty, song says "beautiful" ones, sure. Enter the first nanny problem: a brunette, number nine or ten, who's counting? Four kids, homeschooling, travel, a nanny was clutch. This one? Traveling nanny, not your average sitter. Some accused me of chasing tail–fair, I'm an open book–words blunt as a brick: "Let's fuck" or "Wanna fool around?" leaves no guesswork. Lake Powell, houseboat rocking, thong bikini, damn near naked, strutting past Nichole. Not our norm; others dressed tame. Barely 18, rebel vibe. Nichole had banned booze, but there she was, beach volleyball, sneaking shots. Me? Drunk,

laughing, her fuck-me eyes blaring. I caved, sent
one dumb text: "You wanna do it?" Boom–she's
gone, boyfriend swooping in, standby mode. Text-
ed Nichole my fuck-up and blew it sky-high. Em-
barrassing, I didn't touch her, didn't push, just mis-
read and shot my shot. Nichole? Pissed, rightfully
so–and there we were, Lake Powell, nanny-less,
my mess.

It did feel like a setup; we were seven hours from
home, her flirting thick as honey, and her boyfriend
was waiting on standby? Suspicion brewed in
Nichole; what else had I chased? Truth? Other nan-
nies with our tight-knit traveling family were chill,
no sexual moves. Never hit on 'em, friendly bonds,
not flirty. Then nanny two, chatty as hell, me off
work, Nichole out–she'd linger while the kids
napped, firing questions, endless, probing. Dou-
ble-dated with her and her hubs, drinks clinking,
spilled our swinging past. Her eyes lit up, curiosity
piqued. Alone, she'd dig for answers–sex, swinging, ten billion details–then: "Would you sleep
with me?" Honest? Me: "Probably, in the right
circumstances" but not now, not chasing. I couldn't
win either way–say no, reject her–yes, a shitstorm.

I never fucked her, but she emailed Nichole a novel: "He's grooming me!" Bullshit, anyone I've tangled with knows I don't play coy. She was not my type. Nichole? Livid–two strikes, bold talks–no touching, but me, still torched.

That's the black sheep life, me and my Hap-Penis hat–paints a target. Bold? Misunderstood easily. Maybe if I'd fucked her, she'd have been hush–the Mormon quiet-type–but I didn't, and wrath rained anyway. Accused enough, something snaps– enter Kami. I wasn't going to tease this book with a nanny fuck story and not deliver. I love her–petite blonde fire, baby five's nanny. Our last baby boy, two months post-vasectomy. Swimmers vaulted the cut, Evil Knievel'd the gap–that kid wanted in. Docs said eight weeks no sex–we pushed seven– bam, pregnant. Daughter three piped up, ice cream dripping, "Mommy, you're pregnant." A pregnancy test confirmed, unreal. So Kami? Hot, my type, polygamy's on deck if masks drop. I haven't heard from her lately–that story's wilder ahead.

Life was a fucking whirlwind, an empire swelling, wild and untamed. Remember Parkway Storage?

I went back and bought it, the slave turned king, swallowing the old boss's domain. Overpaid by a million, probably, but I was sold, gut screaming it was right. Added a portable storage arm, tow trucks rumbling, containers shifting, and the empire soared. Nichole's house dreams, sacrificed for years, landed easy now. One house? Nah, how about two? St. George, Utah, the sun-soaked Mormon getaway, snagged one there. Utah County? Nabbed a killer lot to build on in Woodland Hills, sweeping views, sagebrush whispering–until the city pricks balked: "Slope's too steep." Bullshit. I strolled up the block, steeper lots grinning back, homes perched fine. I kept attracting red-tape warriors, or so I thought. I learned later: roadblocks can save you and serve you, sometimes those assholes do you a solid. The market was ablaze and I flipped that lot, $200k netted, butter smooth. My signature move always made the realtor's jaw drop: it's not selling? Hike the price. Too cheap, folks miss the value. That lot languished for months–when I jacked up the price, sold in a blink. Two-acre, dream view lot, gone, cash in hand. Scooped another pad nearby (story for another book) and St. George home two? Locked.

I was rolling, businesses sprouting–too many to track–some soared, some sank, all fun. Cabinet shop, saws buzzing, wood dust thick. Drone company, props whirring, skies humming. Art Mann and I were filming the Testicle Empire, the Drunken Olympics, sexy houseboat bashes, all-out chaos. Good times, except Parkway started dragging like a weight on my chest. Three facilities, dozens of side gigs and help on deck; but costs crushed, bills stacking like bricks. Portable storage? Two tow trucks guzzling cash, repairs, bodies, legal crap from a franchise tangle slowing me. Still, law of attraction clicked, money flowed like water from Testicuzzi, cabinets, chaos. Parkway struggled–an overpriced buy bit me–but we were getting by. Partners, Richard's crew, didn't vibe long-term. I'm 37 writing this–young, hungry, ready to fuck shit up. Them? Old, edging out, chasing cash now, not equity later. I wanted to plow it back, grow–they'd profit, just wait. Calls got heated, then management fees got slashed. Testicuzzi cash had 'em eyeing my wallet, but I was busting ass daily. They didn't see it. Richard pulled early-days stunts, 50/50 flips turned 75/25 and the vibe soured fast. Manifesting sharp, I got my vision board out, scrawled out my goals bold:

- ☒ TEN MILLION DOLLARS ON A SINGLE DEAL

- ☒ BUYOUT PARTNERS, MAKE SURE THEY WIN/MOVE ON

Simple, I thought—shit ignited instead.

Portable storage bled me, my golden touch faltered. Tow trucks started eating profits, repairs, wrecks, and chaos I couldn't tame. The propane refill gig? A sweet girl on staff– the valve popped, sparking a fireball off the asphalt, scorching her and a customer– another childhood acquaintance, what a wild twist. Both healed, thank God, but with an odds-defying fluke, the propane company, fire marshal and investigators were stumped. I was done–DONE–I demanded the gear gone; they dragged, clinging to the idea of more propane revenue. Fuck that, I was over it, no more propane. Parkway vibe drifted the start of it all, was it now the ending? The explosion spooked the partners–

normally storage was easy and clean; propane was a liability. Richard's strain grew, our years fraying.

Home life? The Testicle Empire filming and Kami, the nanny flame, cracked the Walz. Nichole was done with swinging and openness–she'd shut off. Me? I craved it and Kami's face gnawed at me, her flirty sway. Past nanny flak, accusations–it played heavy. Kami wasn't the top-tier nanny, often late and kid-shy, but my interest flared. I shifted her to the Testicle Empire–shoots, parties. Nichole was relieved, and the new nanny in. Kami killed it–wild, sexy, charming, prepping shoots–our work breaks electric. The work gang knew, our playful vibes screaming, but with Nichole's door closed, I clammed up. Openness had been my creed, and now it faltered; the new relationship was building resentment between us. I hid it, which was unlike me. Kami was a joy, filming a dream, fun, our job. Nichole? Cared for, but shafted. Our sex life dimmed, her family's pull widening the rift. I got it–no blame–it's just how it rolled. She thrived at home–me working, traveling–she'd chill with the kids. Our family life though our travels hit just right– Lake Powell, Hawaii, Costa Rica, Bahamas–

affair or not–we rocked it. Kami's new Tundra near
Nichole's birthday? She saw it; she had asked, and
I denied. Our early days' stoplight electric vibe
got buried under diapers, bills, chaos. Love that
sparked kids–lost to them. We opted out of the idea
of public school (no blue-haired rainbow flag-wa-
vers near my kids), ditched vaccines early on. Nan-
nies eased burdens, but crowded the home. Kami?
She was all about me, no kids, pure thrill.

Nichole turned nag–not her fault, mostly mine–
life's a grind, fun fades. Baby five arrived frail,
skinny; he crawled late, rolled slow, lethargic.
Nichole fixated, specialists and worry, but not me.
He's perfect, doing his thing. Her stress and worry
nearly killed her. The affair's reveal? It is a miracle that we survived. Oddly, it opened Nichole
back up for a bit–threesome, trips, just us three, we
worked to repair feelings. Polygamy? It's crossed
my mind; both women are gold. Nichole–my love,
partner, my rock. Kami–a new love, fun energy,
and a fresh sex drive. We bonded and had wild, fun
trips, absolutely–but my kids came first. Kami got
rug-pulled; Nichole's my stoplight wife.

Duty is steel. Our M.O.: full mom-and-dad access, no matter what, all the time. No weekends at moms and weekdays at dads, 100% whenever they want, that stands above all else. Our love from years back, buried under all that insanity, still burns true. We share that desire to give our kids the world they deserve. We love each other immensely for it.

My world was shifting fast, control slipping, or so it felt. I'd been steel-solid, law of attraction walking proof, but doubts crept in like damp rot. Still, I doubled down, chose optimism, bet it'd all work out. Weird shit brewed–not my script, I thought– but damned if it wasn't working, just sideways. Partner calls sharpened, knives out, disagreements spiking. Guys I'd mailed checks to for years–a steady drip of trust–lost the vision. They didn't see the goldmine underfoot, millions glittering.

I took the family to Costa Rica, two weeks, sun-soaked reset, mid-COVID bliss. Empty resorts, staff grinning, tips flowing, treated us like kings. Five-star sprawls, ours alone, kids slurping end-less piña coladas, pool splashing, monkeys raiding snacks from our room. Heaven, vibes high, man-

ifesting loud. Then–brick wall–a call. Some jack-
ass realtor, voice smug, begging for gate codes to
show my storage units. "What the fuck?" I barked,
sand between toes, ocean roaring. "You're con-
fused." He was, and wasn't. Partners, in our rift,
decided my vote didn't count–minority schmuck–
pushing to sell all three as a portfolio. Diabolical,
a $19 million ask. I choked–not just backstabbing,
but underselling–way short. I knew the worth,
they didn't. An overeager salesman's pitch or their
own delusion, I fought back hard: "You're wrong,
price is too low." Then it hit. This was my shot, my
buyout. My manifestation. I offered their ask, full
price, $19 million, they smirked and said "No"--
something about doubting my funding. Fuck that–
I'd bend steel to make it happen. They refused,
took bids, and the betrayal sank in–punishment for
bucking fee cuts.

Their play? Bundle three, undervalue my gem–Marina Cove–at $6 million, when I knew it was $12
million, minimum. Robbery, years of sweat, my
babies, zeroed out. Greedy fucks, refusing my buy
at asking, screamed retaliation. I wasn't folding. I
hired my least favorite breed: an attorney. Dug into

contracts–gold nugget, my find–lawyer nodding.
Marina Cove's structure? Dad—Bob, was listed as
managing member, a silent cash drop, not a finger
lifted. Killed the bundle. God's glitch–why him?
A miracle, I still think. I told 'em to shove it; can't
lump all three. Parkway, Herriman? I was a minority, outvoted and screwed. Marina Cove? Mine–
blood, sweat, built from dirt, not some flip. They
sold the pair, Parkway, Herriman, to a big-box
brand for $14 million. Fools fucked us, $3 million
short minimum, a buyer's wet dream. Richard?
Argued my 33% didn't count, intent bare, years of
draws, $3-4 million profit, settled me under a few
hundred grand. I could've squeezed more, but my
gut said take it. Contract flaw forced 'em; Marina
Cove was mine–all mine. To buy them out, those
slimy fucks went from asking $6 million to $8 million–they squirmed, "You said it was worth $12!"
It was–still a steal–more mine than their portfolio
scam. I saw their side, me resisting cuts stung 'em,
but they weren't grinding: tow trucks, boat washes,
manpower bleeding. My crew deserved raises, not
slashes. That was our first rift in years, odd after
smooth sailing.

But then I closed, had to use a hard money loan, $9 million-ish, 8% interest, fees biting. Hurt, but worth it. I could've nabbed all three, but glad to ditch 'em with something, better than not. Manifestation is twisted, my partners were out, not pretty, but "winning" for them? $8 million over $6 on Marina, $3-4 million from the rest, cash, not cuts. My goal is never lose money and they didn't. Old guard left a bitter taste, but gratitude lingers. The universe paired us, and they fueled me. I'd have found others, sure, but I'm wired for grateful. No real names now, just a sly nickname, a smirking private jab. But I wish them well, and I see that it unfolded for my good–clearer every day.

I was king now, no partner calls nagging, just Bob, good ol' Bob, trust thick both ways. He let me roll; I got shit done. Borrowed $9 million, not $8, extra juice to value-add, always the play. Penny-pinchers gone, orders clear as a bell: build more, make more. Did, another warehouse, more dirt hauled, dust swirling. Not all roses–the city barked, bit, citations piling like junk mail. Government's racket–they need cash? Point the gun, literal muscle. I rolled up to Marina Cove one day, my F350 growling, chrome glinting, to see eight suits waiting: two building dept goons, citations flapping; two fire marshals, smirks sharp; random cronies, cops looming. Stacked it on, occupying no permit, blah blah, power-trip bullshit. This was Pre-Testicuzzi gift basket, but proves my point: we fund their wages, they harass with our own dime. Wild, but I don't dwell; forgiveness is key. I handled it–citations, court, grit–and I stayed king.

Then it hit, should I sell? Utah winters sucked, skiing aside; we chased the sun. $12 million value for Marina Cove, I'd told the old fucks, and had converted that hard money loan to get it into a sweet long-term deal, low interest, lifetime cash cow. I could've ridden it out–but I loved creating, building–so why not cash out, do it again? Enter Austin, my realtor pal, easygoing, solid. He talked me through the old crew's Herriman/Parkway screwjob; he had insider info from that slimy realtors group who was representing the old guys, and had earned my trust. I'd forgot he'd scoped those first dozen units with us–Herriman included–

but he wasn't the lead broker then. Phase 4 done, interest rates dropping, client buzz, and Marina Cove ballooned past $12 million, way past. I had a whim to sell, but it was low-interest lifetime cushion, I told Austin, "Shoot for the moon, list it for $18 million." Same ballpark the old morons valued all three, slimy realtor's bad math, their fear and greed, death looming.

Offers trickled in 16 million, $17.5 million. Held it at 18–I was not budging. Storage? Cash cows, great debt, paid off– I could net $1 million yearly– easy, no expansion. Consolidated, my family was in real homes, not caretaker digs. Life was plush. I nixed the offers, and the real estate market hushed, then I remembered that unbuildable lot with the "too steep of slope". It sat unsold, so we hiked it–cashed out $200k. My Zillow epiphany was that I'd set my filter at $1 million and missed the $990k gems. High-roller mindset, could it be the same in commercial? I called Austin, he seemed pretty down–no bites, his bread stalled. My pitch? "Too low, $21 million." He laughed, "You're nuts". "That's what everyone says," I replied. "Hear me out…billion-dollar 1031 portfolios, tax-dodgers swapping, no gains, no hit." Austin agreed hesitantly; days later, calls flooded, full-price $21 million offer. Hype surged–the universe was winking and Austin's commission fattened. My fence-sitting might seem crazy to some, but for me– it's my blood, sweat, home. Phase 5, 6—$30, $40 million? The new buyer haggled, but I held. $21 million was my line; rates were low, money loose, and I had an appraisal that matched–real, no fluff. Then, we closed. Surreal, done deal. The family greeted me, Nichole kids, Marina Cove tees, balloons screaming "21". This was no accident. Law of attraction hits again.

We settled the accounts, debts cleared–you know how much I netted? 10 million. Exactly. I remembered my notebook scrawl from Parkway, the vision board glaring. Cars, boats, that fucking 10 million deal–odds-defying–dozens of partners had ticked off since, literally robbing me. The old guys? This was confirmation, they'd left $3-4 million on the table with Parkway and Herriman– easy, fear's win. For me it cemented the Law of attraction–those backhoe books on tape, Russian olive scars, no-limits teaching: big shit needs cosmic leverage. Set it, forget it, let go and let God. "Whatsoever ye ask, believing, ye shall receive."

All my sub-businesses were cash sprinkles, not millions. I'd had dozens of partners, 50/50 splits– my cash, their sweat. Generous, I'd never be like Richard–this universe brims with excess, I'd thrive on half. Shocker was, dozens of guys I'd invested with lived in fear, lack, doubt–the tools I'd bought, gone. One guy built a rival shop blocks away, my gear, my hourly pay, chasing 50% equity and he bailed. Uncle Pride–I really do love him–I put him in Testicuzzi at 20%, but 50/50 was written up in my drawer. Pride, one other guy and I were talking about a new side hustle–Pride offered me 15%, not 33/33/33–that's equity shared, an even split. I had bought him a dirt bike as a bonus, meals, fat Parkway fees, but in my mind he showed me: fear mode, greed mode. Days away from giving him Testicuzzi papers at 50% and I switched to 20% instead; it was better than the 15% he'd offered me in the other deal. Pride's genius shines, he got 20%--we drifted, but we're good, we still work together, this story news to him. The universe showed what was mine–50/50 flopped if they didn't believe. Hard days, undercut partners, bailing in fear, but me, I'd always hold fast–it will fucking work.

Chapter 8:

The Lone King

Kami and I had been outed, Nichole and I were sorting, honestly, polygamy teased. Bahamas yacht, Kami and me, Nichole at home, cool with it, kid-free. The trip was great, but that energy, that bond Kami and I had, it dimmed. The new openness weighed. Families–hers, Nichole's–branded me the villain; they saw my wild, fully exposed. Nichole's sister, aptly known to me as Satan, red-headed hell-stoker, played up baby five's frailty against me. Facebook has a secret women's page–anonymous–all for man-trashing. My mug got posted, and Satan fed it to Nichole. Tinder lies, bullshit, no proof–Nichole now knew all my truth–Kami was out in the open. Satan's meddling–that bitch threatened to snatch our boy for a doctor's appointment–snapped Nichole and me. A fight erupted, and you know what tipped it? Satan: she fueled my fire, no one–and I mean no one–threatens to meddle with my baby. Well, the Walz's were caving in, divorce loomed. Kids' world crumbled, tight-knit no more. Satan's fuel, I'm certain a jealous bile, spiked it. Why'd she meddle? Nichole always outshone her–prettier, funnier. Satan wore the college badge which was no match for Nichole's grit. But Satan wanted bridges burned. All I could think about was Parker's lesson: "What if I don't wanna partner?" Satan well, she seemed to love the blaze–fuck her underworld bitch fits.

Chaos erupted, all that money swirling, and Nichole's family chanting divorce like a war cry. I couldn't shake it, was all that new cash a factor? Her folks didn't seem that twisted, but Satan, redheaded venom, texting Zillow links for neighboring pads Nichole could snag? A big "kumbaya" on my dime–there was fucking angle there. That bitch was relentless. Papers were filed, depression slammed, hard. My five babies, shattered, sob-bing spontaneous wails, moping loops, daggers to my heart, deeper than anything I'd ever felt. Emotions? Not normally my game–but now, rage, sadness, boiling over. All that optimistic, manifesting bullshit was crumbling now, my world was imploding. How could Nichole, that selfish jerk, divorce me, do it to our kids? The truth hit: not just her, not just me–relationships are a shared mess. No excusing my affair, but she can't pin all the crap on me. It's a team effort, for better or worse, the end staring me down like a shotgun barrel cold against my face. We'd built it, wealth unimaginable, Ferrari growling, G-Wagon purring, Tesla humming, boats, houseboat, toys piling up, five-star globe-trotting. All meaningless now–no family, no joy. Money? Gold when life's good, resentment fuel when it's ash. No gift could hush my kids' cries; all they craved was Mom and Dad, in the same room, hugging it out–forgiveness, compromise, love, us–whole again.

Bob stepped in, he always cheered our wins, ached our losses. Torn, he and Michelle dropped everything, raced to St. George. Hours spilled, me sob-bing, kids dying inside. We had a sit-down: Bob and me, Nichole and her mom; Nichole was an icy wall, a shell of herself. Her mom spat, "Knock off, it's done." Nichole was silent, her only jab: "Your charm's dead this time." I saw a glimmer there–a stab at me, sure–but "charm"? An echo of old days, her on my side, ditching Mormon facades for real, raw talks, life unfiltered. She was done…but not fully. It felt like 1% odds. But that's my wheel-house. Hope flickered and Bob's marathon talks, ironically using Neville Goddard–the good old law of attraction ammo I'd fed him. Have faith, belief, feel it–but it was too raw– the odds 99% against. Nichole was locked behind her family's old ways, fortress tight.

I called an old Mormon mentor–an attorney, solid guy, nixed speeding tickets before. He spilled it; got a peak behind the other attorney's curtain; war brewed. He dug for clarity from Nichole's law-yer–ugly, brutal. "Do this, do that"--he sent me in defense mode, my brain fogged, I clung to his lead. But the hole deepened, and I saw clear as day, the law of attraction flipped: positivity breeds more;

negativity snowballs. My vibe was complete garbage now, manifesting ruin, grander than my wins. Attorney pal, echoing Austin, and dozens before, called me nuts when I wanted to give in: "Don't do it, or I can't rep you." That was fuel–crazy's my badge. Divorce papers loomed, yet remained unserved, and I saw it: fighting custody and cash bred more fights. Bob's Neville Goddard words burned: *envision the family whole, and the universe delivers.* There was nothing to lose, so I ponied up, and locked in. The physical world is my canvas–I'd repaint. I told the attorney to politely "Fuck off." In the St. George home, not on a notebook, but on my knees, I hit the ground–instead of paper, I wrote on my heart: "Whatever I ask, believing, I'll receive." I fucking meant it, steel in my soul. Normally I sleep solid, even with chaos looming. I've taught myself there's no such thing as chaos, but this time, 4 a.m., I jolted awake. All I could hear was, *California.* It made no sense–St. George had pools, kid pals, good vibes. Kids loved Cali, we'd visit often–San Clemente, Laguna Beach, Dana Point, all quaint, electric, fun lands nearby. The kids woke and it was unanimous: "California

129

sun, Dad, it's right." Nichole was in Salt Lake, I explained the distance to the kids, and the potential issue with going farther. The kids seemed bothered; they felt a sense of betrayal–this was not mom's hug-it-out norm. They felt it too–but there was this tiny spark of inspiration. Our nanny at the time an absolute angel–not a fuck buddy–but a gift from heaven; she soothed their tears through my sobs. She can vouch, the kids decreed: "Mom'll meet us there, she wants us." I still teetered, the custody talks were fragile, so going to Cali felt like a big risk. But the kids' approval sealed it. We hit the road, California dreams just hours away, dawn breaking.

Bob locked in the same prayer written on his knees, etched in his heart. He described it vivid: Ryan, Nichole, five kids, huddled tight, a heap of love, peace, forgiveness, thriving as one. He saw it, I saw it–and we handed it to God. Nichole came, she followed that California sun calling. She did not share my bed, not even the same house. She stayed in the next-door rental, that was her line in the sand. That was fine; her presence thawed the kids' torn hearts, normalcy creeping back. It was rough–14 years, open-hearted conversations every day–and now, her words scarce, the air thick with weirdness.

Satan was always absent when we soared, but suddenly, she craved the sun, all in the name of making sure my charm didn't work its magic. She showed that misery really is her fuel, eternal flaming bitch. The days stumbled awkwardly, we we're trying to map a new future: side-by-side houses, that was better than miles apart. It echoed old talks, kids get 100% of us, differences be damned. That was the Nichole I knew, soft, open, shit-test champ of the world. Each day that went by shaved that 99% impossibility–still, she held firm: "It's different now, we'll work the rest out in court." Next-door life, family dinners, it was close enough for me. Funny, when she'd leap back to the old family Mormon ways, that divide was our saga; my flowers, chocolates, gifts could be flipped to an evil view–it was manipulative, that was her old Provo west-side lens: the rich guy squandering, fake Santa, money pissed away. But the East side of Provo taught me; positivity is a choice. The Park-

way Storage bosses', their stick analogy, there are
two ends, always there, our focus picks which side.
Flowers? They can be love's dream, or manipulative fuckery. It's our call–that taunting duality is
our burden.

One night–a knock on my door, glass framing her,
Nichole–defeated, drowning with the heavy side
of the stick. I didn't care, I knew our vow: better
or worse, forgive, love, chase the good, even when
it's fucking brutal. She opened fast, climbed in
bed, silent, no sex, just her hand in mine, like old
days reborn. My tears streamed, I hoped she hadn't
seen. At that moment, I teleported to St. George,
knees on the ground, Jesus' genius blazing: "Whatever you ask, believing, you'll receive." $10
million? That was peanuts. This miracle trumped
all. Family hugging in the living room–five kids,
Nichole, me–that's priceless, my responsibility, my
point of attraction.

Jesus nailed it, worthiness is us, born in all children of God, not mimicry, but action. It's the trick
of ages and no church is required. Call it God,
Universe, Angels–doesn't matter–just believe, then

see. I started my church, Saints of the Future, no pews, no walls, just an idea. Gospel of Christ, the law of attraction, only share when it fits–not for salvation, no force. No tithing to steeples, only tithe to God, to self; there is faith in receiving. Then when you receive, share with neighbors, friends, only when it's right. No prophets; we are all equal, worthy wherever. Love? Non-negotiable, you gotta love, even the haters. Their venom? Your mirror, we all have work to do and I've got plenty on my to do list–Satan's proof. Banished from her lair, but she's not banished from mine. I can't hate–it's not truth, not how the universe rolls. I call her Satan for kicks, but I wish her well–anger's my wound. But Jesus' gem: turn the cheek, it's the only way. It's not ego's flex, but an inner trek, what you reap, you sow. Satan? Well, that's my wrestle. I'll get there.

Years on, and Nichole and I hold strong, adventures and stories for new books, you seriously wouldn't believe, taking on bankers, attorneys–fuck, even governmental authority. Plenty of new problems tackled, and our differences exist. She balks–Kami as wife number two, next door, that's my idea; neither's sold. What matters is that the family hugs roll. I'm good–kids, they are my angels.

The point of spilling my guts in this fucked-up, wild-ass book? My proof, rock-solid evidence of how the law of attraction runs the show. I'm not just here to slap Testicuzzi on the world–though that's a hell of a mark–I want to etch something deeper. Authors before me–Hicks, Dyer, Goddard–they lit the path, showed me the way through their words, crackling tapes in a backhoe cab. Now, in my twisted, pervy, one-of-a-kind spin, I'm passing it on. That's the game: learn, grow, share, each of us taking our shot. This isn't about preachy bullshit or some holy pedestal; it's real, messy, lived. If Saints of the Future, my church idea, vibes with you, join up. Easy, everything living is welcome–no gatekeepers. No steeples, no confession booths, just us, walking the streets, heads high, living it. Might kick off some gatherings, whacky, wild, maybe even sexy, or just bonfires in a field, tents flapping, drinks clinking, fuck if I know. Never about big-church flex–giant buildings can suck it. The core? Faith in your own pull–believe in it, grab it, share it when it fits. No dogma, no dues, just you, the universe, and a middle finger to the old ways.

This ride–money, chaos, family, betrayal, miracles–it's all me owning my law of attraction. I built an empire, lost partners, fucked up, won back love, every step, my lens shaped it. You have the same power. It doesn't matter where you're at, clean slate or shitstorm. Pick your side of the stick, focus there, and watch it roll. I've seen it: $10 million deals, kids' hugs, impossible odds flipped. Not magic–it's you, it's me, it's us. So, camp out with me in some muddy field someday, or just nod from afar–either way, you're in if you want it. Let's burn the old script, stack some wins, and laugh while we're at it.

All are welcome!

SCRIPTURES THAT BACK ME UP

"Judge not, that you be not judged.

Matthew 7:1

"Let him who is without sin among you be the first to throw a stone"

John"8:7

"For by your words you will be justified, and by your words you will be condemned."

Matthew 12: 36-37

" The Father judges no one, but has given all judgment to the Son"

John 5: 22-23

"Be merciful, even as your Father is merciful, Judge not, and you will not be judged: condemn not , and you will not be condemned"

136

Luke 6: 36-37

"But I say to you, Do not resist the one who is evil. But if anyone slaps you on the right cheek, turn to him the other also."

Matthew 5: 38-39

" Love your enemies and pray for those who persecute you."

Matthew 5: 44

Ryan's Rules for Success

1. ***Own Your Shit, Scars and All***
   You don't get anywhere pretending life's polished. I've fucked up—nanny scandals, partner betrayals, family on the brink—and I own it. Success comes from staring down the mess, NOT HIDING it. Your story's your power.

2. ***Believe It, Then See It (Law of Attraction 101)***
   I scrawled "millionaire by 30" as a kid, felt it in my bones, and hit it. That $10 million deal? Vision board gold. Focus on what you want—cash, love, whatever—feel it real, and the universe delivers. Doubt's a dream-killer.

3. ***Let Go and Let God (or the Universe)***
   Dirt for Marina Cove showed up when I stopped chasing it—Vegas trips, good vibes, bam, trucks rolled in. Stressing kills the flow. Work hard, then chill. Trust the bigger force to sort it.

4. *Positivity's Your Fuel, Negativity's a Trap*

Broke folks bitch, rich ones dream. I flipped chaos into millions with optimism. When divorce loomed, I chose hope over rage—family hugged it out. Pick the good end of the stick, always. Every situation can be seen like the stick, one side better than the other, you pick up the stick (your life's situation) it always comes with both ends, you choose which side to focus on.

5. *Hustle Like Hell, but Delegate Smart*

I swung hammers, scrubbed toilets, built empires—but you can't solo forever. Hired a manager for Herriman, freed me to scale. Grind 'til you bleed, then build a crew who bleeds for you, teach them so they can also rise above.

6. *Shit-Test the World*

Testicuzzi? A nut-soaking gag that sifted tight-asses from the bold. My Hap-Penis hat does the same. Throw out wild shit—see who bites, who balks. Winners join the party; losers fade.

7. *Forgive the Assholes (Even When It Stings)*

Sent a gift basket to that prick building manager—permit showed up next day. Partners screwed me? I let it go, wished 'em well. Hate festers; forgiveness clears the path.

8. *Cash Buys Freedom, Not Happiness*

Jeep roaring, steakhouses, hot dates—money
unlocked it all young. But when kids cried
in divorce chaos, millions meant jack. Stack
it, use it, but know what's real.

9. *Break the Rules That Don't Fit*
Mormon guilt, church tithing, mission pressure—I ditched it. Saints of the Future? No
steeples, no dues, just belief. If the system's
bullshit, burn it down and build yours.

10. *Learn from Titans, Then Outgrow 'Em*
Parker's jet-rich lessons, Scott's business
riffs, Dee's sales gold—I soaked it up, then
leapt past. Mentors light the fuse; you're the
rocket. Don't stay in their shadow.

11. *Price High, Win Big*
Woodland Hills lot sat dead—jacked the
price, sold fast. Marina Cove at $21 million?
Moonshot, closed. Cheap screams desperate;
bold pricing screams value. Another manifestation of fear is under valuing.

12. *Love Hard, Even the Haters*
Nichole, kids, even Satan—I can't hate.
Jesus said turn the cheek, and it's steel:
love's NON-NEGOTIABLE. Venom's their
wound, not yours. Keep the door open.

13. *Take Inspired Action, Don't Just Dream*
Popcorn for Oklahoma, backhoe through
olives, Testicuzzi from a joke—I did it, not

just thought it. Ideas are air; action's the hammer. Move, fuck up, learn, repeat. Find yourself feeling like you are losing?, change the action until you re algin with positive action. Action when positive will have positive results. Action from negative will have negative results.

14. Empire's Co-Creation, Not Solo
Subcontractors, Nichole, Bob—Marina Cove rose on their backs too. You're the king, not the kingdom. Share the load, share the wins.

15. Fear's the Enemy, Faith's the Blade
Partners bailed, scared of equity over cash. I bet on belief—$10 million proved it. Fear keeps you small; faith cracks the ceiling.

For more on the Saints Of The Future visit:

www.SAINTSOFTHEFUTURE.org

For more of Ryan's Projects:

www.THETESTICLEKING.com

For your own Hap-Penis hats and apparel, visit:

www.TESTICUZZI.com

use code TTKBOOK for 20% off Hap-Penis merchandise.

YouTube

The Testicle Empire

www.ingramcontent.com/pod-product-compliance
Lightning Source LLC
Chambersburg PA
CBHW051716090426
42738CB00010B/1936